Pitkin's P.A.
MY LIFE WITH
Sir Norman Wisdom

By

ANN AXE

with

Sue Benwell

Lily Publications

Lily Publications
2010

ISBN: 978-1-907945-02-1

Published by:
Lily Publications Ltd
PO Box 33
Ramsey
Isle of Man
IM99 4LP

This edition © Lily Publications Ltd 2010.

www.lilypublications.co.uk

Typeset in Adobe Garamond Pro.

ACKNOWLEDGEMENTS

Ann and Sue would like to thank the following people for their help during the writing of this book.

Colin Bishop
Morris Bright
Dina & Todd Carty
Alan Clarke
Tony Clarkin
Miles Cowsill – Lily Publications
Bill Dale
Phil Day
Peter Elliott – Brinsworth House
John Gatenby
David Graham
Yvonne & Tony Hateley
Jeff Hill
Johnny Mans
Doug McKenzie
Mix96
Michelle Montuori
Ian Smith
Wesley Smith – BBC Radio Oxford
Jeremy Spake
Enid & Malcolm Watson
Sir Norman Wisdom's family -
Jacqui, Nick, Kim, Lawrence & Greg

AND, not forgetting the man himself, of course…

Thank you, Sir Norman!

A proportion of the proceeds from the sale of this book will be donated to some of Sir Norman Wisdom's favourite charities.

Contents

Norman with Todd Carty and Todd's son James.

Foreword

by Todd Carty

To write anything about Norman Wisdom, you could go on for months, let alone years, with story after story. Norman was a legend in his own lifetime, praised by Charlie Chaplin as his favourite clown. And even managed to save the Rank Film Organisation from financial failure with a clutch of his classic films. Starting with one of my personal favourites, *Trouble In Store*. Norman even managed to beat James Bond at the box office, he was that popular.

When Dina was pregnant with our first child James, she had me sing to her tummy one of Norman's songs from *Trouble In Store*, 'I'd like to put on record that I love you love you love you'!

Norman paid regular visits to our house in North London and Dina would often cook him one of his favourite childhood dishes, shepherds pie. And whenever we would go with Norman for a fish and chip supper in Muswell Hill, Norman would literally stop traffic as we walked around the broadway. Norman had the ability to bring the child out in everyone, he had universal appeal. All ages would call out his name and others would crowd around him for a chat or ask for autographs. Norman brought smiles to people's faces as soon as they set eyes on him.

On one occasion, outside the Odeon Cinema, Muswell Hill, we saw a traffic warden across the road, about to put a ticket on my car. Suddenly he looked over and on seeing Norman, he had a big smile on his face and shouted, 'Norman Wisdom, I can't believe it, my favourite actor.' And he added, 'No ticket for you today mate!' The only name he took was Normans autograph.

And while at any restaurant, Norman would like to start a food fight with my boys James and Thomas, ending up with all of us involved. I recall another occasion at a major west end do, Norman throwing food at the Albanian Ambassador and other people from high office, causing quite a stir. Only Norman could get away with that.

At a restaurant table, Norman would often ask, 'Do you like sea food', and would open his mouth with the contents of his meal on his tongue, saying, 'See – food!'

While we walked down any street, Norman would ask, 'Where is the nearest car showroom', he simply adored cars. And he would approach people as they stood by their car asking, 'Are you selling'! And as they gazed at Norman, taking in who he was, he proceeded to check the car over, he was in his element. And it always ended up in laughter, with his trademark trip or funny comment or two.

At the car showroom, Norman wasn't interested in the sedate family type of car. But the fast powerful cars such as BMWs, Mercedes, Jaguar, motorbikes, all high performance vehicles.

Norman simply loved speeding, be it walking, running or driving. His energy levels were that of a man half his age, there was no stopping him when he got going.

When Dina would ever announce what time lunch or dinner

would be ready Norman would always ask me, 'Let's go for a drive, it won't take long', and he always gave that knowing look, Once I said, 'Let's go Norman', he was into the car like a shot, ready for action. Norman never liked to sit still for long, even as he grew older, he was forever young. And as we drove down a long winding road such as Totteridge Lane and then into the Hertfordshire countryside. Norman would urge me to drive on for miles, 'Dina won't mind Todd', he said with a twinkle in his eyes.

After meals, Norman would sit on what we called, Norman's chair, an old Victorian armchair which Norman liked and always chose to sit on. And we would watch all his films over time, which brought back so many memories to Norman. And he would recall every detail of every scene in every film, like it was only yesterday. It was great to listen to his many stories about his filming days. And to hear Norman explain such classic and funny scenes, such as the stretcher scene in Mr. Grimsdale's butcher shop and the falling on top of an ambulance scene from the same film, *A Stitch In Time*. As well as the tumbling down a flight of stairs with a cup of tea in hand without spilling it, from *The Early Bird* and other classic scenes like the police chase in *On The Beat*. And so many others, you could listen to Norman for hours, or watch his films again and again and still laugh out loud. My children had the best of both worlds, laughing at his films and the man himself. Being with Norman was sometimes like being in one of his films.

When we paid Norman a visit to the Isle Of Man, he made us feel so welcome. He loved to show us around his house and his beautifully kept gardens and a tour around his beloved Isle of Man. 'What smashing scenery' he would say and Norman would take us to the great beaches on the island. We liked to call it 'The Isle Of Wisdom'.

Norman was up to his usual tricks when we arrived and would direct us down a dead end road and got a great kick out of it, as he watched us get confused.

There are of course many stories I could tell you about our time with Norman. He was never showbusiness like and was always a natural, down to earth humble man. He always used to say, 'Im a lucky little devil'. But he deserved all the success he got through pure natural talent and a total belief and all out enjoyment as an entertainer and above all, a great actor. Norman entertained millions all over the world through his work on radio, stage, television and films. And he will continue to bring joy and laughter to millions more who get the chance to see his great work in his classic films. He could act, sing, dance, play so many instruments, tumble, mime, laugh out loud like no other and at the same time, he was a friend to my family and we will never forget our magic moments with Norman. God bless you Norman, your legend lives on. And thanks Norman for all the happy memories and joy you brought into our lives.

Todd Carty

1

Introduction

July 2007

"Where are we going, Ann?" asked Norman, from the front passenger seat of Maureen's car.

Maureen met my gaze in the rear-view mirror and now raised her eyebrows at me, imploringly. Both Maureen (Norman's ever-faithful housekeeper) and me (his trusted Personal Assistant, I'd always liked to think, anyway) had suffered many a sleepless night worrying about how best to deal with this impossibly painful situation.

"It's so unfair," I mouthed at her reflection.

What had this dear man, who brought sunshine and laughter to the lives of millions, ever done to deserve such a cruel affliction?

That morning, I'd taken Norman breakfast in bed, as per my usual routine.

Each day it alternated between his favourite cereal and porridge, but this particular breakfast consisted of a bowl of cereal, a cup of *very* sweet tea, along with a brightly coloured multi-vitamin pill in the saucer.

Norman always woke up happy. In all the years I worked for him I had never known him to start the day in a bad mood. More often than not, the sound of his beautiful singing voice would drift down towards me as I negotiated the stairs.

That morning, though, all seemed ominously quiet.

Balancing the cereal bowl and cup and saucer precariously in one hand, I tapped on his bedroom door and entered: "Normi! Breakfast!"

Norman was still in bed, his eyes tight shut and his head lolling over to one side.

Placing the breakfast things on his bedside table, I pulled back the heavy drapes and bright sunlight suddenly flooded the room. "Oh, come on, Norman," I said, with an exasperated sigh. "You know that we've arranged to go out with Mo today."

Norman's mouth drooped to one side in a horrible, death-like gape.

I folded my arms, feigning disinterest. "I'll leave your breakfast on the side, then, shall I? Don't let your tea get cold," I added, turning to go.

One mischievous blue eye opened, quickly followed by the other one. "Fooled you!" he shouted gleefully, pointing an accusing finger at me.

"Oh, Normi," I chuckled. "How many times have you played dead over the years?"

My insides gave an unpleasant lurch, as in that awful moment I realised that he might never be able to play his endearing prank on me ever again.

Norman's gardener, Rodney, and his wife, Pam, came over during the morning, to snap some last treasured photographs of him at home. Normi, of course, was in his element, pulling silly faces at the camera.

"Just look at him," I said, fondly. "He has no idea, has he?"

"How many other distractions will we find for him to do, just so that *we* can avoid the inevitable?" whispered Maureen, with a heavy sigh.

At one o' clock precisely (Norman was a stickler for punctuality) we sat down to a lunch of his favourite foods: Bangers and mash with onion gravy, followed by sponge pudding.

"Here's another of your favourites to finish off, then," I said, handing him a steaming mug of milky coffee.

"Ooh, thanks." If it had crossed his mind that he was being especially fussed and spoilt that day, he never commented.

"We've strung it out for long enough," I said to Maureen, finally. "Now, for our afternoon *drive*."

"I bag the front, Ann!" shouted Norman, climbing into the passenger seat.

"You always do," I answered, getting in the back.

Norman's beautiful home was situated on The Lhen, about two miles from Kirk Andreas on the Isle of Man. Appropriately called 'Ballalaugh', or, 'Home of the Laugh', it always lived up to its delightful name whenever Norman was in residence.

As we pulled out of the driveway on that gloriously sunny afternoon, I knew the once vibrant house would be a lifeless shell without his impish, fun-loving presence.

Increasingly forgetful, Norman had been blissfully unaware of all the covert activity going on around him. He hadn't even enquired about the whereabouts of many of his familiar knickknacks, including a couple of chairs. They had already been squirreled away to his room at the nursing home by his dearest friends, Malcolm and Enid, in an attempt to make things more comfy and familiar for him.

That was the main reason Mo had volunteered to use her car, it was big enough to secrete yet another bulky item out of sight in the roomy boot.

Mo took us on an enjoyable drive around the Isle of Man's narrow, leafy lanes, but for two of us, at least, the trip was both wonderful and heartbreakingly sad in equal measure.

"Oh, look at that!" Norman shouted excitedly, even though we had seen the charming row of cottages umpteen times before. The next minute, winding down the window and frantically waving at some bemused tourists as if he'd known them all his life: "Cooee! Lovely to see you!"

We rounded off our afternoon's jaunt over on the west coast with a delicious Davison's Manx ice cream at Peel, the island's only 'city' and one of Norman's favourite places.

We all sat in silence for a while, eating our cornets while sitting on a bench looking out over the sea and Peel castle.

"This is the best ice cream I've ever had!" Norman announced, before daubing some of it on the end of my nose and then laughing like a naughty schoolboy.

"I knew the peace wouldn't last," I said, wiping away the rum 'n' raisin-flavoured blob with a tissue. I hadn't the heart to remind him that we'd actually eaten ice cream, gratis, from that very parlour on Peel promenade, almost every week for as long as I could remember.

"You reopened the parlour for the Davison's when they refurbished it in 2005, didn't you, Normi?"

"Yes, that's right," prompted Maureen. "You really enjoyed the day, didn't you?"

Norman just looked at each of us in turn, with no hint that he had any recollection of the happy event, and then carried on eating his ice cream.

After the re-opening, George kindly sent us a delivery of four large tubs of differently flavoured ice creams. When I phoned to thank him, he'd said: "You will still bring Norman in here for his cornets, won't you?"

Yes, everyone loved him.

Now, though, it was my exceedingly solemn duty to hand him over to the caring staff at Abbotswood nursing home.

Norman first gazed up at the two-storey building and then turned in his seat to fix me with his keen, blue eyes. "What is this place, then, Ann?"

"Um," I answered, swallowing the huge lump in my throat.

"Why have we stopped here, Mo?" he persisted, tugging at her sleeve, but she turned away from him, desperately trying to keep a lid on her emotions.

For the first time since I'd started working for him in 1994, I told him a blatant lie. "Norman… I… I… need a little break for a few days and so I… we've… that is, your family and I, have booked you into this… um… h… hotel. Nice, isn't it?"

"Are you staying here with me, then?"

"No… um… I have to go back and check that everything's okay at the house," I replied, lamely.

He shook his head: "No, no, I'm not 'avin' this. Stop messin' about, Mo, and start the car."

"We can't renege on the booking, Normi, or we'll get into trouble." It didn't sound very convincing, but I couldn't think of anything else to say just at that moment.

"I wanna go home."

Unfastening my seatbelt, I leant forward and placed a reassuring arm around his shoulder. "Oh, Norman, please don't make things any harder than they already are. Come and see inside, at least, and then we can have a nice cup of tea."

"I dunno," he shrugged.

"Come on, I've got a chocolate caramel in my bag."

"Oh, all right," he agreed, reluctantly.

"I will come back tomorrow to take you out for the day," I assured him, aware of how hollow my voice sounded in the confines of the car.

"You promise?" His eyes were beseeching.

"I promise."

"Well, okay, then, just this once."

I would keep my word about the day trip, but Norman would surely never trust me again.

Sun, Sea and Sand

October 1993

Genoa's busy Italian seaport bustled with frenzied activity and a huge, white ocean liner dwarfed the ant-like people on the quayside.

Divorced and in a dead-end job, I always found that Solo Cruise Holidays were a good way of meeting some very nice, like-minded people. Not just guys on their own looking for a bit of romance on the high seas, but other ladies in a similar situation to me.

Making my way through the throngs of people, I suddenly felt some urgent, woodpecker-like taps on my shoulder: "You'll never guess who's in our party," one of my fellow female passengers babbled, excitedly.

"Who?" I called back to her, over the clamour.

"Norman Wisdom! He's always been one of my favourites."

"Yes, he's very funny," I agreed.

A smile crept across my face, as I recalled watching his hilarious antics on telly when I was young. My sister Joan and I had gazed adoringly at the screen, both falling in love with his endearingly vulnerable 'gump' character.

In later years, when I was in the merchant navy, I did see one of his films, which was A Stitch in Time, I think, but hadn't actually followed his career that closely.

Still, I mused to myself, *he's a bit of a showbiz icon, so it will be fun to bump into him.*

I didn't have long to wait!

Relieved of my luggage, I hurried towards the embarkation point, where I very nearly collided with him. "Ooh! Ooh!" yelped my latter-day idol, spiralling round on one leg, despite the fact we hadn't actually made bodily contact.

"Oh, I'm t… terribly sorry, Mr Wisdom," I stammered, by now feeling decidedly embarrassed, as other passengers were walking past and laughing at his antics.

His face suddenly launched into a smile and he shook my hand. "Hello!" he said, his 'injury' miraculously forgotten. "I'm Norman, who are you?"

"Hello, um, Norman," I answered, with uncharacteristic shyness. "I'm Ann Axe." I waited for the usual jokes about my surname, but none were forthcoming.

Instead, he just regarded me with two of the most amazing blue eyes I'd ever seen. "Well, Ann, it's very nice to meet you and I hope that we shall be able to spend some time together, during the next three-and-a-half weeks."

The ship set sail and after dinner that evening, I headed up on deck. I was just leaning against the guardrail, gazing out over the darkening sea, when I heard a kafuffle going on behind me.

Turning round, I saw Norman and another gentleman hurriedly making their way towards me. Grabbing both my hands, Norman looked like a lost child who had just found his mother.

"I couldn't find you at dinner," he sobbed, convincingly. "I thought you'd gawn overboard."

His companion grinned and introduced himself. "Hello, I'm Patrick, Norman's old army buddy and I must apologise for my friend's behaviour. Can't take him anywhere," he chuckled.

"Cor!" said Norman, eyeing me up and down appreciatively. "That's a smashin' dress."

"Why, thank you," I answered. "And you are very smart, too."

With his full head of freshly washed, silver-grey hair, Norman looked really dapper in beige trousers, a light-blue top and a sports jacket, so much so, that it was astonishing to think that he was well into his seventies.

Norman leant forward and sniffed the silk corsage pinned to my dress. "Must be ha… ha… hay fever," he said, giving a theatrical sneeze.

"Bless you!" shouted a nearby group of guests in unison.

Placing a protective arm around my waist he then steered me over to join them. "'Ere, you lot! Come and listen to this." We were kept amused for the entire evening with songs from a tape that he had just recorded called The Musical World of Wisdom.

The ship's first port of call was to be Madeira and I was really looking forward to actually setting foot on the picturesque island, as I had sailed there many times during my stint in the merchant navy, yet never been ashore.

I was just checking through the day's intended itinerary, when I felt a sudden tap on my shoulder.

"Do you realise that this area is out-of-bounds, Madam?" said a male voice in a clipped tone and I spun round, quite expecting to see an officer in uniform.

Instead, there stood Norman, looking very nautical in white shoes, white trousers and a navy top. He was also wearing a white hat with the word 'Captain' emblazoned in gold letters on the front.

"Oh, it's you, Norman," I laughed. "Where on earth did you get that hat?"

"In the ship's shop, or is it the shop's ship? He said, pushing at his front teeth with his thumb. Adopting the posh accent again, he added. "Tell me, dear lady, when we dock, would you do me the honour of accompanying me to the Reeds Hotel for tea?"

"Oh, thank you for inviting me, Norman," I said. "But I've already agreed to go ashore with someone else."

"What! Not that bounder I saw you with at breakfast, I hope?"

"No, I… "

"I warn you, if you spurn my advances I'm liable to jump orf this ruddy ship."

"Oh, Norman, I'll join you another day… "

This did nothing to dampen his ardour, however, and he ran towards the guardrail.

"Norman! Get down!" I yelled, as he dangled precariously over the churning, spume-topped waves below.

"Only if you promise to join me for dinner tonight," he answered, petulantly.

I wagged my finger at him. "Now, you know the rules, Mr Wisdom. You have to move round all the tables so you get to dine with everyone."

"Not when you like somebody, you don't," he replied, jumping nimbly back down onto the deck.

Suffice to say, for the rest of the trip, our little trio became inseparable and we would move around the various dining tables, adhering to tradition, as a job lot of three.

Norman couldn't even behave himself in the plush Dining Saloon, however.

On one occasion, he found himself sitting beside a tiny woman with mouse-like mannerisms. "Look over there!" he told her.

The poor lady placed her small, round glasses onto the end of her twitchy little nose and glanced over to where he was pointing. "What is it?" she squeaked, only to turn back and discover that Norman had heaped some of his dinner on to her plate.

I think he was concerned that she needed feeding up a bit. "Wonder if she'll order some cheese for afters?" he whispered to me.

Most evenings the three of us would settle down to a game of scrabble and Norman was ecstatic when he came up with the word, 'quiet': "Look at that!" he said, proudly. "Bet you can't do better."

His face was an absolute picture when it came to my turn and I added "est" to the end.

Norman must have forgiven me, because the next day he took me along to a drinks reception in the Captain's cabin. The ship was a beautiful big, old vessel, with huge cabins and wide corridors.

"I feel so at home on here," I said to the captain.

"This is the old Kenya Castle," he explained.

"Yes, I was on the Transvaal Castle when I was in the

merchant navy, so this was one of the Union Castle's sister ships."

Norman stuck the tip of his little finger in the corner of his mouth. "Yes, but what ever happened to their brother ships?" he quipped, in his best Margaret Rutherford-style voice.

True to my word, I accompanied Norman and Pat on various excursions around the Caribbean islands. Filing back on the coach after these visits, our driver and tour guide would take a head count of passengers.

Until it came to Norman's turn.

He would loiter around until the last moment, smile pleasantly at the driver, place one foot on the bottom step, then turn on his amazingly athletic heel and sprint off. Nobody ever minded, though, because he made us all laugh so much.

They might not have been so forgiving, of course, had we driven into the harbour, only to see the ship sailing away into the sunset, minus a coach load of (AWOL) passengers!

Norman loved to have an unhindered view of the countryside and so quite often bagged the front seat next to the driver.

This, though, also gave him the opportunity to sometimes snatch the microphone from our beleaguered tour guide, meaning, of course, that we would then be treated to one of his completely incoherent talks about all the various points of interest en route.

On another occasion, a car suddenly stopped dead in front of the coach and the driver had to stamp hard on the brake pedal.

Norman flew down into the stairwell with an alarming thud and everyone on board gasped in horror. I was just about to rush to his aid when he suddenly popped up, sporting crossed eyes and dishevelled hair.

During these trips I realised just how stubborn Norman could be: "What's so special about a Gruen watch?" I asked him, after he'd made us traipse around the shops in the heat for hours trying to find one.

"It's a copy of a Rolex," he explained.

"Well, why not simply buy a Rolex?" Pat reasoned.

"Coz it's a lot cheaper than a Rolex," Norman replied.

I should guess that most people reading this would by now have come to the same conclusion as Pat and me!

Norman's stubborn streak did pay off in the end, as he managed to find one on the penultimate island we visited. In subsequent years he used to joke to everyone that it was a Rolex, until, eventually, he truly began to believe the story himself.

We went out on the Rum Run, which was an afternoon's excursion on a boat, where they served as much rum as you could drink.

"This is a… rum do." Norman hiccupped to the mouse-like lady.

You can appreciate why the poor woman clung on to her meagre plate of food (*and* glass of rum) for grim death.

In between these excursions, we attended many of the afternoon tea dances in the regal theatre-cum-dancehall. Norman was a snappy little dancer, but if a wicked glint suddenly appeared in his eyes, something was definitely afoot, so to speak.

"I know," he whispered, conspiratorially. "Let's fall over."

"Norman, you're the comedian, *you* fall over," I told him.

At the sound of a sudden commotion behind him, the bandleader's baton stopped in midair. Norman sprawled through the legs of the other dancers and the music ground to a tuneless halt, perfectly emulating a scene from his movie, A Stitch in Time.

During one of these dances, a funny little man butted in for an "excuse me".

"Oh, thank you," said Norman, coyly pretending that he thought the man was requesting a dance with him, not me.

After a momentary muddle, Norman finally pirouetted away with the man's wife. I had a job to keep a straight face, when I spotted him striding up and down the dance floor with her, abruptly changing direction every few steps, as if they were dancing to some sort of manic version of the tango.

I think it was meant to be a slow waltz, if my memory serves me correctly!

I even have a treasured photo of Norman trying to steal a deck chair.

"'Ere, 'ang on a minute!" he yelled at the well-muscled, non-comprehending German tourist. "Give it back, I only went to fetch me drink."

The pair of them ended up having the most hilarious tug-of-war, Norman trying to walk away with the chair, his white plimsolls skidding and squeaking on the deck like some sort of Michael Jackson moonwalk.

Every morning at 10.00am there would be a two-mile walk or run (depending on your fitness level) around the deck. Quite a few of our English contingent used to join in, with a crewmember counting your laps so that you knew you had completed your two miles.

I would smile at everyone as I jogged by, until one particular morning, when I noticed that people were actually laughing, instead of acknowledging me with a courteous nod like they usually did.

(I thought, *well, Charlie can't be dead, coz I'm wearing shorts and a tee shirt*).

I stopped and turned round, just in time to see Norman running along the deck towards me, if 'running' is the correct word to describe his over-exaggerated, rubber-legged performance.

"Oh, Norman, whatever are you doing?" I chided him.

He stopped beside me and did a bit of shadow boxing, much to the delight of his growing audience. Then, he ran past me, tripped over his feet, did a perfect roll, jumped up and continued on his way, to the spatter of appreciative applause.

I was also highly amused to learn from our hostess, Carol, that he had even visited the gym.

"How did you get on, Norman?" I enquired.

"Like that," he answered, pretending to straddle an imaginary fitness cycle.

"Can't you ever be serious?"

He began to fiddle with his nails. "I didn't get on very well... actually," he added, his lower lip quivering.

"Oh, dear, why was that?"

"Well... I... sank the rowing machine."

With the cruise coming to an end, the ship headed for its final port of call in Caracas, Venezuela, from where we were due to fly home.

"Norman, thanks to you, this has been the most enjoyable cruise I've ever had." I sighed, happily. "I've got a permanent pain in my side through laughing so much."

"As long as it isn't a pain in the neck," he answered, razor-sharp as always.

"You know, if your secretary ever needs a break, I'll gladly work for you."

His expression suddenly became serious for a change. "Do you mean that?"

"Yes, of course I do."

"Well, what would you do with your house?"

"Sell it!" I answered, decisively.

Isle of (the funny) Man

The following spring, I went to see Norman in his hilarious "Live on Stage" show in Worthing.

Arriving at the theatre in good time for the 7.30pm performance, the taxi driver dropped me off right outside the Stage Door. Admitted into Norman's dressing room, I noticed that the shelves were laden with 'Good Luck' cards and several huge vases of flowers.

"Norman, how lovely to see you again," I said, kissing him on both cheeks. "You look as if you've been running up and down the stairs," I added, suddenly noticing the beads of sweat on his furrowed brow. "You aren't going down with a cold or something, are you?"

He merely grunted in reply.

"I see you haven't changed at all in the past five months," I laughed, thinking he was just joking around and would suddenly perk up. For once, though, he didn't join in with my laughter.

To be honest, the atmosphere in that dressing room was like wading through treacle and I began to wish that I'd simply stayed away and committed all thoughts of my wonderful cruise to memory.

"I... I'll see you later on," he said, ushering me out.

I felt a bit deflated and spent the entire evening wondering what I might have done to upset him.

The laugh-a-minute show was hugely enjoyable, though, and Norman (and his comedy stooge, Tony Fayne) received a standing ovation at the end of it. Marvelling at Norman's stamina, I was worn out simply watching him from the auditorium.

Afterwards, full of admiration, I waited in the corridor outside the dressing room while Norman chatted to his family.

Suddenly, Norman's Personal Assistant, Barbara, appeared at my side and steered me over towards a couple of chairs. "Ann, are you busy?" she whispered, as we sat down. "That is, have you got any ties?"

"Barbara, if you ever need a break, I've told Norman that I would be more than willing to help out."

"It's more than that," she said. "I really need to leave. I've already been back once and I've got a lot happening at home, with Mother not well."

"I see what you're saying, Barbara, and I'd love to help, but Norman seemed quite off with me earlier."

She laughed out loud. "Oh, he's always like that before a show. Actually, he doesn't normally see *anyone* beforehand because it's considered unlucky, so you were very honoured."

Whoops! Not the best way to rekindle a valued friendship when you hadn't seen someone for a while. "Thank goodness for that," I sighed with relief.

Barbara squeezed my hand. "I know I'm asking a lot, but how about coming to see us at Norman's flat in Epsom when we finish this tour in a fortnight's time? We can discuss things in more detail."

"Okay, yes, I'll look forward to it."

In the dressing room I was pleased to find that Norman was back to his usual ebullient self again.

Over the next few days, I began to doubt whether Barbara would actually contact me. True to her word, though, she phoned me about a fortnight later and we arranged to meet the following Thursday.

What took place could not be described as an interview, really, more a friendly chat over a cup of tea, when it was agreed that I should fly out from Gatwick, all expenses paid, for a week's trial at Norman's home over on the Isle of Man.

*

Norman was waiting for me at Ronaldsway Airport, where he at once took control of my suitcase.

Everyone laughed, as he strutted through Arrivals and then waltzed around all over the place like some sort of demented porter.

"Well, if you think that I'm giving you a tip after that performance," I told him, loud enough for my fellow travellers to hear. "You've got another thing coming."

Outside, he ushered me towards one of his cherished babies, a Nissan 200ZX, and opened the front-passenger door with a flourish. "Please take a seat, my lady."

Once I was safely ensconced inside, Norman scurried round to the back, where he tried in vain to lift my suitcase. "Wot yer got in 'ere, house bricks?" he shrieked, when it remained resolutely 'stuck' to the tarmac.

Suddenly, a real porter dashed to his aid. "Can I offer any assistance, Mr Wisdom?"

Needless to say, before the poor confused man could grab the handle, Norman hoisted up the case as if it were feather-light and placed it effortlessly into the boot, dusting his hands triumphantly.

As we sped along the narrow lanes, the serene beauty of the island quickly became apparent to me. "It seems a world away from the bustle of the mainland. I can quite see why you moved out here, Norman."

"Yes, I fell in love with the island in the late seventies, whilst appearing in a 3-month summer season at the Gaiety Theatre in Douglas," he explained. "The pace of life is definitely slower and the Manx people have a very appropriate saying about it," he added.

"What's that?"

"Traa dy liooar."

"Oh, yes, and what does *that* translate to, exactly?" I asked him, expecting to hear some sort of wisecrack in reply.

"It means, time enough."

A bit later, I found myself looking at an impressive, grey-stoned house.

"What do you think, then?" Norman asked me, as he turned the car in to the driveway and pulled up outside 'Ballalaugh'.

"It's beautiful," I told him, admiringly. "You must be very proud."

He walked round to my side of the car and opened the door. "Yes, I am, especially when I think back to my childhood, stealing scraps of food from market barrows in London."

We entered 'Ballalaugh' via a wide hallway and then continued on through some curved glass doors… opened, of course!

"This is stunning, Norman," I said, gazing round. "Oh, and

this looks so tasteful," I added, looking down at a lovely Chinese mat, placed on top of a pink carpet.

Inside, there was a magnificent sweeping staircase, with a banister on one side and a rope along the other, against the wall. Although there wasn't any kind of a vaulted ceiling, it was open right up to the very top of the house, which made the entrance hall seem delightfully bright and airy.

Barbara greeted me warmly and led me into the lounge. "Have a seat, Ann," she said, pointing to a Spanish-style settee. "I'll make us all some coffee."

My eyes were immediately drawn to an oil painting of Norman as Aladdin and then to a huge corner display cabinet, chock-full with his numerous showbiz awards. The room itself was large enough to comfortably house Norman's much-prized grand piano, a magnificent French Erard.

"See that piano stool?" he said. "It used to be a coffee table."

"Are you having me on?" I laughed, waiting for the punch line.

"No, straight up, although the legs are not straight up, they're bowed," he chuckled, before coyly sticking his tongue in his cheek. "No, seriously, the legs matched the piano's and so I had it adapted."

"How ingenious."

"Do you recognise the stone fireplace?" he asked

"Yes, I do, isn't it like the one in your flat?"

"Well spotted! I had them both specially made, although the one in the flat is much smaller, of course."

Hanging above the fireplace, amongst many other collectables, were two pistols and a bayonet, which seemed a little incongruous in this otherwise jolly "home of the laugh".

Norman suddenly stretched out his hands in a gesture of surprise: "Go on, Ann, try and guess where the telly is?" he said, widening his eyes in expectation.

I glanced around the room. "I've no idea, but I suppose the easy chairs and settee must be facing in the general direction."

"Quite right!" Norman opened a door at the side of the fireplace and out popped a huge television.

"That's very neat," I said.

"Well, there are no wires on show, as I can't stand to have spaghetti junction cluttering up the floor."

Norman sat himself down in one of two luxurious armchairs and Barbara rejoined us, placing a tray of steaming mugs on a big, round, mosaic table.

After coffee, Barbara showed me over the rest of the house and the only fault I could find with it, if I'm being picky, was a very badly designed kitchen. Oh, there were plenty of work surfaces and loads of space, but the cooker and sink were in opposite corners!

There was a little study next to the kitchen, with heaps of fan mail very much in evidence on the desk, then a door leading through to the sunroom and, from there, another door, out into the manicured back garden.

Upstairs, there was the guest bedroom, where I would sleep, as well as a small bedroom, which was Barbara's.

Norman's bedroom was positioned right at the end of the landing and enjoyed the same gigantic specifications as the lounge. There were two red chairs and a double bed, along with a full-length mirror, some plush floor-to-ceiling drapes, a dressing room and an en suite bathroom.

Norman and I just posing for the camera.

Norman and entertainer Michelle Montuori on board the cruise ship Van Gogh.

Norman demonstrating how to fall off a bench in the gardens of Pinewood Studios.

Norman and I on the deck of The Americanas – bound for Caracas in Venezuela.

Stopping for a rest with Patrick behind the camera.

Norman in The Canaries practising his football.

Patrick, me and Norman having a day at the beach on a lovely island.

Norma Fane, Norman, Tony Fane, me and Patrick sailing on the Black Prince.

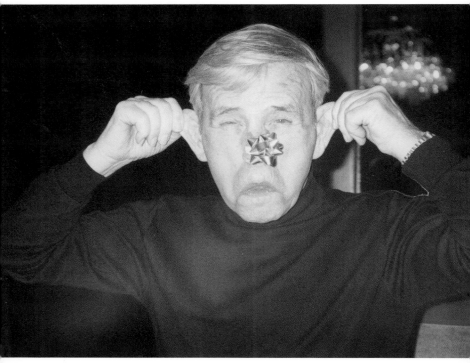

Pulling faces as usual.

Esther Rantzen Show.

Norman practising his songs with pianist Emile on board the cruise ship Van Gogh while I wait patiently for them to finish. This is after I return for the final time.

On set for Last of the Summer Wine when Norman played Billy Ingleton.

Norman with the cast of Last of the Summer Wine at Pinewood Studios.

Norman with Howard Keel in Liverpool at a luncheon in the 90s. They had not met since The Royal Variety Performance in 1954.

This is the so called signed photograph for Very Cheeky. I just hope no one ever takes him seriously!

At another dear friend Ruth Gemmet's house where we spent many happy hours. Here we are with Ruth's lovely son Dominic who has cerebral palsy. Norman has known them since Dominic was a small boy.

Norman waiting to be called to give a speech at Pinewood Studios having a moment's deliberation.

With Thora Hird at the same event.

Chatting to his statue when it used to be in the main shopping area in Douglas.

Somewhere on his beloved Isle of Man.

Norman and I with his beloved 1956 Bentley Continental Fastback.

A typical Norman Wisdom photograph at his home.

Norman visiting an aquarium somewhere in the Caribbean.

This was in the Isle of Man. I did say to him, 'don't pull a face, be serious'.

On the Amsterdam cruise in 1994 being entertained by some magic.

Tony Hateley, Norman, me (the caddy!) with their golf team in Spain.

In celebration of

Norman Wisdom OBE

and his films made at
Pinewood Studios
1953 - 1966

reserve and Foster the Tradition of British Comedy

The British
Comedy Society

*Norman with Tom O' Connor, Dame Thora Hird, and Sir Donald Sinden in
Pinewood's Hall of Fame.*

Norman at his flat in Epsom, just prior to his 80th birthday.

"What else can I tell you?" pondered Barbara. "Ah yes, Norman likes routine and is fanatically tidy."

"I gathered that from looking around," I said. "Everything is spotless."

"It's from his army days. Well, do you have any questions, Ann?"

I thought for a moment, before asking: "It seems very quiet here, so what do you find to do in the evenings?"

"Oh, our evening routine consists of watching the telly - mainly sport or Norman's videos - well into the early hours."

"Oh, I see," I answered, a little taken aback. Not being much of a night owl myself, I made a mental note that if I did stay on at 'Ballalaugh', then there would definitely have to be some changes… if only to prevent the place from becoming known as 'Ballasnore'!

The next morning, Barbara and Norman decided to take their usual bike ride, a five-and-a-half-mile circuit that included a visit to the paper shop at Kirk Andreas.

"But what will you do, Ann?" asked Barbara. "We haven't got a spare bicycle."

"I will jog along behind you," I said, pleased to be able to keep up with my fitness regime.

It was so nice to see the countryside at a much slower pace than the previous day's Jeremy Clarkson-style drive. After the pre-planned stop at the newsagent, all seemed perfect for a time, until I rounded a bend and noticed that my two companions had disappeared from sight.

By now, having grown used to Norman and his tricks, I half expected them both to leap out on me from behind a hedge and, slowing down to a walk, I peered gingerly along a likely looking farm track. "Come on, Norman, I know you're hiding."

Nothing!

"Right, Ann," I said out loud, stopping to glance round at the endless fields and unfamiliar lanes stretching away into the distance. "Looks like you've gone and got yourself lost on your first day."

First Impressions

Next morning, I threw back the blankets and padded my way to the bedroom window.

"Don't know what you're tiptoeing for," I chuckled to myself. "By the sound of it, Barbara is up and about already."

I drew one curtain aside, gazing out over the immaculate lawns, flowerbeds and mature trees, to where two young rabbits nibbled at the short grass. "What a view," I breathed, as my eyes were drawn towards the distant hills.

My bedroom door suddenly clicked open, making me jump: "Morning, Ann!" said Barbara.

"Ooh, Barbara, I was just enjoying this lovely view."

"Yes, it is very beautiful," she agreed. "You can see the summit of Snaefel up the top there. Norman and I must take you around the island whilst you're here, Ann, so you can get your bearings. Did you sleep well?"

"Yes, I did, thank you," I answered, stifling a yawn.

"Anyway, would you like to join me in the kitchen in a bit and I'll show you how Norman likes his breakfasts prepared and then we can take him breakfast in bed?"

"I'll be right down."

Whilst dressing, I mulled over the previous day's adventure, when getting lost had taken me on an unwarranted, six-mile, sightseeing tour of the island.

I'd eventually arrived back at 'Ballalaugh' to find Norman and Barbara embroiled in an important, pre-arranged meeting with one of his charity colleagues, both of them intent on organising a search for me, though, at the end of it.

Oh, dear, not a very auspicious start, I thought to myself, vowing to do better in future.

It did seem quite surreal, though, to be staying in the home of one of Britain's best-loved comedians. I suppose people might have said: "How on earth did you manage to *swing* that one, Ms Axe?"

Yes, well, perhaps it would be best if I leave the joke telling to Norman!

At eight-thirty sharp, Barbara tapped on Norman's bedroom door and I followed her inside, carrying his breakfast.

"Good morning, ladies," he said, brightly. "I hope I'm going to be spoilt rotten today with the two of you fussing around me."

"You should be so lucky," answered Barbara, cuffing his arm, playfully. She went over to the window to draw the heavy curtains, then plumped his pillows and tucked a napkin under his chin, as I handed him his bowl of porridge.

"Thank you, Ann. I see you found your way up here all right, then?"

"Yes, I've got a map in my pocket," I rejoined.

Back in the kitchen, Barbara told me about Norman's usual daily routine: "He's a stickler for time, as I mentioned before, Ann. He has breakfast at eight-thirty, lunch at one, then supper when we get back from our afternoon drive, which may be as late as eight in the evening, sometimes.

"Oh, and a milky coffee and biscuits at ten-thirty every morning, with whoever's on duty at the time, be it Rodney the gardener, or Maureen the housekeeper.

"After your busy life, Ann, it probably all seems a bit mundane," she shrugged, finally.

"On the contrary," I assured her. "I like to keep to a routine, too."

Barbara told me about Norman's favourite foods, which included bangers and mash, casseroles, meat pies, gammon with dumplings, in other words, anything plain and hearty that would stick to his ribs, like Pease pudding.

Next, I followed her through to the office. "As you can see, Norman gets loads of fan mail and likes to answer every letter, personally," she said, with a sigh. "Trouble is, though, there aren't enough hours in the day and it soon mounts up."

"Is that what you use?" I asked, nodding towards a couple of ancient typewriters.

"Yes, I suppose we are a bit backward, technology-wise," she agreed, picking up on a note of disdain in my voice.

"You'd get through it in a fraction of the time with a computer," I said, thinking about my own computer and printer, redundant on the desk back at home in Southsea.

A bit later on, I peeked around the door into the drawing room, where Norman was now engrossed in his newspaper. "You look nice," he said, looking up.

I refrained from answering: "Oh, what, this old thing?" and simply thanked him for the compliment, as I'd bought the smart top and trousers in a snazzy boutique, especially for my visit.

"We'll have to keep an eye on you today," he added, with

a wink. "We don't want you trying to escape from our clutches again."

"I can see it'll be a while before I'm allowed to live that down," I laughed.

"Oh, yes," said Barbara, joining us. "You can be sure that Norman will certainly get some mileage out of it for a good while yet."

*

The Liverpool to Douglas ferry pitched and rolled during the choppy, afternoon crossing.

With all my years at sea in the merchant navy, the petulant Irish Sea seemed quite benign, but I did notice a few fellow passengers hurrying towards the facilities with their stricken faces turning several shades of green en route.

During the four-hour journey I nibbled some sandwiches, drank coffee, and read Norman's autobiography, '*Don't Laugh At Me*', using the time to swat up on my new employer.

I suppose that some people might think that all the 'breakfast in bed at eight-thirty sharp' and 'lunch at one' palaver was just a bit of starry indulgence on Norman's part.

Yet, reading between the lines of the book, it seemed obvious to me why Norman loved to be looked after and pampered by his female assistants.

His mother had abandoned him at a young age, leaving him and his brother in the care of a violent father, meaning he'd missed out on so much during his early years. The strict adherence to routine would simply be a throwback to his army training.

If I'm totally honest, I did have mixed feelings about my

adventure to the Isle of Man.

Yes, I was well travelled and used to living away from home during my younger days, but setting out to spend a long stint on a tiny island to care for a man I hardly knew, did seem to be rather foolhardy in some respects.

Living in Southsea, I'd grown used to seeing my family on a regular basis and I loved my house, the interior of which I had designed myself from top to bottom.

I also owned two little poodles, Tramp and Hobo. Norman loved dogs, yet it didn't seem fair to expect him to take them on, especially when I'd only just started working for him.

Thankfully, my son, Wayne, who had been sharing a house with four friends, had kindly offered to go back home to housesit and dogwatch for me.

I'd made a list of all the pros and cons of the job, but eventually came to the conclusion, *hey, what the heck, it's not etched in stone and there's no law to say a woman can't change her mind if things don't work out. Anyway, nothing is certain in life and perhaps Norman might have some misgivings about me, too.*

Disembarking at Douglas, I drove down the ramp, turning the car north towards Andreas.

If the ferry company had decided to impose weight restrictions on vehicles, then mine would have been well and truly over the limit.

Suffice to say, that with several suitcases, plus a variety of bags containing extra clothes and much-loved photos and knick-knacks, not forgetting my computer and printer stashed on the back seat, there was no room for the kitchen sink!

*

'Ballalaugh' was like the Marie Celeste when I arrived there at six-thirty that evening.

I knew they could not have gone far, because the coals were illuminated on the electric fire and, sure enough, I then heard Norman's car crunching up the driveway.

I have to admit that he did look a little nonplussed when he saw me. "You here already?" he said, giving me a welcoming hug.

"I told you I was catching the two o' clock ferry."

"Yes, but the way you ladies meander around the lanes, I thought you wouldn't get here till at least eight."

"Bloomin' cheek! I'll have you know that I'm quite handy behind the wheel, Mr Wisdom, and I certainly don't *meander* anywhere."

"Didn't get lost on the way here, then?" he asked, trying to wrong foot me.

"Norman, I happen to love cars and fast driving, just as much as you do," I told him.

Barbara looked a little bemused. "I can see that you two are going to get along just fine when I'm gone," she laughed.

That first week flew by in a whirl of visits to various friends on the island, like Malcolm and Enid, and, Di and Adrian, who ran the Chablis Restaurant in Castletown.

I was also taken to see some of the better-known beauty spots, such as the huge Laxey Wheel, where Norman happily mingled with the holidaymakers.

"What's it for?" I'd asked, staggered by the sheer size of the thing.

"It's for training," Norman told me, his eyes blue twinkling.

"Training what?"

"Giant hamsters!"

"Oh, really, Norman," Barbara scoffed. "Don't listen to him, Ann. It's the largest water wheel in the world and was used to pump water out of the mineral mines."

At the end of the week, Norman drove Barbara to the airport and my memory is a bit hazy at this point. I cannot for the life of me recall whether I accompanied them to the airport, stayed at home, or, if they simply dropped me off at a friend's house.

All I know for sure is that I didn't want to intrude on their final goodbyes.

For the sake of argument and in the interest of moving the story along, I shall say that I accompanied them to the airport, with apologies to Barbara if I've got it wrong.

"I know he's in trustworthy hands," Barbara said to me, misty-eyed. "Are you sure you won't come and see me off?"

"No, no, I'll wait here in the car," I told her.

Norman was unusually quiet when we returned home, so I tried to make small talk over lunch. "At least Barbara's got a fine day for flying," I said, without much of a response. "Did she get off all right?"

"How should I know if she got off all right," he piped up. "She's not even home yet?"

"I meant, did she get off all right on her journey *from here*, as you well know," I laughed.

"They'd never arrive at all if you were navigating the plane," he muttered.

I started to clear the plates. "Yes, yes, very funny."

"They'd probably end up in Timbuktu."

"Humph! Have you quite finished?"

"Yes, thank you for the lunch," he answered, getting up. "You don't cook in the same way as Barbara."

"Listen, Norman," I broached. "I know you're sad about Barbara leaving, and that's quite understandable, but I will try my best to fill her shoes."

He looked around the room. "What! She hasn't left her ruddy shoes here again, has she?"

"I can see I'm getting nowhere fast," I sighed.

"Ha!" He waved an index finger at me. "No change there, then!" With that, he grabbed a newspaper from the magazine rack and tucked it underneath his arm. "Cheerio!" he said, brightly. "I'm off for an afternoon nap."

"Well, that went well," I said, unsure quite what to make of our exchange.

Barbara phoned later on in the evening.

"Glad you got back okay, dear," I told her. "I'd better pass you over to Norman, as he's jumping up and down here, waiting to speak to you." I handed him the phone and retreated to the kitchen.

Slotting our supper plates into the dishwasher, I suddenly overheard him say: "Oh, come on, Barbara, when are you coming back?"

I slammed the dishwasher door, making the crockery rattle like chattering teeth. "Right, Mr Wisdom!" I whispered, defiantly. "I'm going to turn this place around and be the best bloody personal assistant there's ever been."

First Class Male

I hardly had time to glance at Norman's fan mail during that first week.

Now, letters and postcards of all shapes and sizes, including some with brightly coloured stamps from far-flung destinations, vied for my attention on the office desk.

Norman dictated the first few replies to me, but kept slipping between past tense and present tense, which made things unbelievably confusing when I came to type them up.

"Right, Norman," I said. "This is far too laborious. We are going to tackle this in a methodical way and you will see how much easier it is, replying to them all on the computer."

"Can't we just stick to the typewriter?" he complained. "I don't know how to use one of those new-fangled things."

"Well, luckily, this is something I *do* know my way around," I answered, triumphantly, quickly setting up a template for 'thank you' letters.

"That's clever," he conceded, as I ran off a copy for him to sign. "But won't it be a bit impersonal if you just reel them off like that?"

"No, because I can change the text on screen, as appropriate," I explained. "Anyway, you can always add a handwritten postscript if I've missed anything out," I told him. "I'll tell you what, to make things easier, I shall clip the sender's original letter to each one and you can write an appropriate and more personalised note at the bottom."

Norman checked through the contents of the first letter and signed it with a flourish. "You're a s… hot secretary," he nodded, appreciatively.

I afforded myself a secret smile and then asked him: "Is there a stationery shop on the island?"

He thought for a moment. "Well, the shop round the corner keeps fairly still."

"Oh, Norman, be serious."

"Why do you want a stationer? We've got tons more paper in there," he said, pointing to the bulging filing cabinet.

"Yes, but we really need to organise a more eye-catching logo for you."

I did find a local stationer, taking with me a little caricature of Norman, which they placed beneath his name on the letterhead. I also arranged to have a batch of 'with compliments' slips printed up and these had the same caricature, only bigger.

I then gave Norman a simple lesson on the computer, teaching him how to save letters and do easy alterations to the text. "Cor! It's better than that old typewriter with its faded ribbon, isn't it?" he agreed, finally. "There is one thing I don't like, though."

"Oh, what?"

His lower lip trembled. "I miss the 'ding' sound when you get to the end of each line."

There were still lots of things to do, quite apart from all the fan mail, as the long table behind my desk was covered in holiday brochures and other paraphernalia, whilst every office drawer, overflowed. Gingerly opening the door of a large cupboard, I was suddenly rained on by hundreds of car magazines and long-forgotten scripts.

"Curiosity killed the cat," Norman chortled.

"I shall have to sort it all out," I told him, with an exasperated sigh. "I can't work in such a muddle."

I packed everything into large bags and Rodney the gardener kindly helped me to store them away, up in the loft area at the rear of the garage.

Dealing with the mail everyday, I discovered just how loyal Norman was to his fans, or 'chums', as he called them. If anyone wrote and asked him to ring a family member for a birthday surprise, then he would always endeavour to honour their request.

Inordinately kind, he put himself out and made time for people. "Where would I be without my chums?" he'd say.

Most of his fans were lovely, although he did have a couple of over-zealous ones who became somewhat fanatical about him. After me having a little heart-to-heart chat, things did improve and they were harmless enough.

On the kitchen front, I soon adapted a lot of Barbara's recipes round to my way of working. For example: Barbara would poach tripe and onions in milk, whereas, I'd make a roux, adding some of the redundant booze languishing in Norman's cocktail cabinet.

He hardly ever touched alcohol, apart from a sweet sherry with Sunday lunch, and so I thought I should make use of this untapped commodity. My yummy gravy became the stuff of legend… well, at 'Ballalaugh', anyway!

The practical, everyday things were starting to gel nicely and

Norman was very slowly beginning to embrace the changes.

On my part, I suppose that homesickness, coupled with the fact I missed my family, did make me feel a little bit touchy at times, when Norman's jokes could easily grate on the nerves.

Imagine walking into a seemingly empty room, only to have someone jump out from behind the door and frighten you half to death. Yes, it was funny the first time and, maybe, the second or third time, perhaps.

By the tenth time, however, his harmless prank had really begun to lose its appeal, especially when it caused me to drop a cup of tea all over the carpet.

I remember one day, creeping around the house like a fool, checking in all his usual hidey-holes as I went. I fully intended to scare him for a change and was incensed to glance out of a window, only to see him sitting on the garden bench quietly reading his newspaper.

"Norman! You're turning me into a right fruitcake," I said aloud.

He also had the annoying habit of sneaking up behind me when I was preparing vegetables at the kitchen sink. "Bo!" he shouted on one occasion, suddenly digging me in the ribs for added effect.

"Norman! I nearly stabbed myself with the potato peeler."

He picked up the colander, stuck it on his head and danced around the kitchen like a whirling dervish: "Ooh, I've got a brain like a sieve!"

"Put it down, I need that," I scolded, although I knew that chastising him was a total waste of time, as he would never temper his craziness for my benefit.

My 'me' time was early morning, when I'd go for a six-mile bike ride before breakfast while Norman was still in bed. It was quite safe to leave the front door on the latch, go for my ride and then let myself in again, ready to make Norman's breakfast.

This worked fine, until one morning when I accidentally locked myself out.

"Drat!" I said, or something along those lines.

I cycled off into the dawn, figuring that Norman might have surfaced by the time I returned, but all was quiet when I got back. "Norman! Norman!" I shouted from the back garden, until his tousled head appeared in the window.

"Yeah! Wadda you want?"

"Can you let me in, please?"

"No, go away, or I'll call Mr Grimsdale."

"Oh, come on, Norman, stop messing about."

"Not today, thank you."

"Don't you want any breakfast, then?"

I apologised profusely to him when he eventually opened the door, yet he didn't complain, bless him, and just went back to bed.

Anyone reading this might think: 'What a lazy man, staying in bed everyday', but it was simply the showbiz habit he'd adopted when touring, as late nights on the road always meant long lie-ins every morning.

After my daily bike ride, I'd spend an hour or so in the office before preparing Norman's breakfast. Once I'd done my exercise routine, I could then have a shower and go back in the office until coffee time at 10.30, which meant that I soon managed to knock the fan mail into shape.

Norman phoned Barbara every Tuesday: "When are you coming back?" he'd say. Now, though, he would glance across the room and wink at me, so I must have been doing something right!

The Early Birdie

Our first proper excursion away from the island was to the Norman Wisdom Charity Golf Classic in Manchester.

I drove to Epsom, via the Douglas to Heysham ferry, and we spent a couple days at Norman's flat before setting off to Mottram Hall. After the long drive north, we finally pulled up outside the impressive 18th Century hotel, near Prestbury.

"What a lovely place, Norman," I said, looking up at the colonnaded front. "Oh, look, here comes... the... door... man."

Before I had a chance to finish the sentence, Norman was out of the car like a whippet and dashing round to the back. Lifting up the boot lid, he began to "fight" over our suitcases.

"'Ere, give me that!" he shouted. "Mr Grimsdale, he's stealing me cases."

This mock tug-of-war between the two men continued on through the door of the hotel and into the luxurious foyer, where I had visions of a suitcase bursting open and lacy underwear being strewn over the shiny floor tiles for all to see...Norman's, that is, not mine!

Norman suddenly stopped his nonsense at the reception desk. "Good afternoon, Miss," he said to the receptionist, in a posh voice. "My name is Mr Wisdom and this is my secretary bird, Ms Ann Axe."

What would you do with him?

We eventually made it to our respective rooms without further incident and I was just placing a few items on hangers in my wardrobe, when there was a knock on the door.

"Can we swap rooms, please?" asked Norman. "This is so much nicer than mine."

"But your room is exactly the same as this one, surely."

"Nah, this is...cosier," he said, glancing round. "The bed is a bit smaller."

"Oh, Norman, I've just put all my clothes away, now."

His eyes began to swim with tears. "Oh, please, let me have this room," he pleaded, grabbing my hand and going down on his knees. "I promise I'll be good for the rest of the weekend."

"I doubt that very much," I told him. "Oh, go on, then," I relented, finally.

He rained kisses on my hand. "Oh, thank you, thank you," he cried. "You dear, dear, lady."

"All right, there's no need to milk it, Wisdom."

This was something else that I learned about Norman: Despite the fact that his bedroom at 'Ballalaugh' was of palatial proportions, he preferred to feel cosy when he was away from home.

After breakfast the following morning, I joined Norman on the practice greens before the start of the afternoon's tournament.

It was a total waste of time, because, as you might expect, he spent the entire morning fooling around rather than perfecting his swing, although we did manage to sort out which were to be his favoured clubs for the game.

"Is this a sand wedge?" I asked him.

"No, it's a bag of crisps," he answered.

"Norman, if I'm going to be your caddy, I really need your help, here," I remonstrated. "You know this course, so which of these clubs do you normally use?"

"I should think a Jeremy 5, and… a cheese and pickle, amongst other things," he said, with a superior sniff.

I racked my brains. "Oh, you mean a 5-*Iron* and a *sand wedge*, yes, right, very funny."

"Not forgetting a traction engine."

I tried to think of the possible answer to this one, but eventually had to admit defeat. "Sorry, you've lost me, now."

"A TRACTION ENGINE… a putt, putt, putt, PUTTER," he emphasised.

"Oh, of course, silly me. I should've known. Ah!" I added, triumphantly. "I suppose you might also need an Epping."

Norman looked at me askance. "An Epping?"

"You know, an Epping Forest… a wood!" I laughed, pleased with myself to have at last contributed something to this strange conversation.

"Now you're just being plain daft," he answered, dismissively.

After lunch, we headed out to the first tee to join Norman's golfing partner for the game, Tony Hateley. A lovely guy, who was, allegedly, the most transferred football player, ever.

Norman stared theatrically off down the fairway, his hand shielding his eyes from the bright sunlight.

The Tannoy crackled into life and I must confess to being none the wiser as the disembodied voice informed us: *the*

*Norman Wisdom Golf Classic will be played as the best 2 from a
4 ball Stableford.*

"This is a 450 metre, par-5 hole, Ann," Tony told me,
handing me the course card and a pencil.

I just nodded meekly and extracted an *Epping* from
its neighbourly slot next to a *Cheese and Pickle* in Norman's
golf bag.

I cannot for the life of me remember Norman and Tony's
opponents on that occasion, but other celebrities who had
agreed to play that day, work commitments permitting,
included the likes of: Frank Carson, Dennis Taylor, Norman
Collier, Stan Boardman, Gareth Hunt, Bobby Davro, Jasper
Carrott, Stephen Hendry, the list went on and on.

Norman lined up his shot, thwacking the ball so hard that it
flew down the left-hand-side of the fairway.

"Bad luck, Norman!" said Tony. "You're in the rough."

Sprinting over there, Norman scurried around trying to find
his ball and it was hysterical to see tufts of long grass and weeds
flying into the air.

He then ran out onto the course in front of his opponents
just as they were about to play their second shot. "Cooee!" he
waved. "I'm lookin' for me ball."

Running back into the rough, he appeared again a
moment or so later, carrying it triumphantly in the air. "I
found it, Mr Grimsdale!"

Naturally, it wasn't really his ball. Just one he'd taken out
of his pocket in order to shock everyone into thinking that
he had broken the game's strict code of conduct.

At the end of play, Norman put on a bit of a show for

the spectators. "What on earth are you doing, Norman?" I said, as he proceeded to lie down on the grass. "Get up at once."

Ignoring me, as per usual, he positioned the putter (or rather, the traction engine) along the ground.

He then pointed the handle-end towards the hole, finally sinking the ball effortlessly into the cup with a snooker-style shot that even Stephen Hendry would have been proud of.

Later, Paul Gaskell hosted the Celebrity Charity Dinner. "Norman will help me present the prizes," he announced and a knowing murmur went around the room.

Norman clambered around amongst the many items on the stage, sometimes teetering dangerously close to the edge and frantically wind-milling his arms.

"'Ere! Catch this," he shouted, literally throwing the prizes, such as fragile boxes of Waterford Crystal, down to the terrified recipients. He almost threw a TV at one guy, but, thankfully, common sense prevailed, although I think that poor Paul nearly suffered a coronary.

Snooker aces, Dennis Taylor and Willie Thorn, did a good job with the charity auction, despite Norman's comical interventions.

Norman and I raised loads of money, selling raffle tickets at £10 a pop. It might seem expensive, even by today's standards, yet we kept running out of tickets, as everyone was so generous in their support of Christie Hospital's Cancer Fund.

The golf classic over for another year, Norman was then booked to pay a visit to the Gainsborough Golf Club in Thonock, home of the Ping Academy.

We had to cut right across the middle of the country to Lincolnshire, but the journey was well worth it, as Gainsborough was a stunning place, with two 18-hole golf courses: one, a traditional parkland course, and the other, an American-style layout.

They presented Norman with a full set of Ping custom-fit golf clubs and kindly gave me a half a set, too, which I thought was very generous of them.

On a more personal level, the trip to Gainsborough turned out to be quite fortuitous for other reasons: "While we're up this way, Norman, I'd like to show you where I was born," I said.

"What! You mean the actual bed and everything?" he said, horrified. "Is the midwife still alive after all this time?"

I refrained from sloshing him one and headed up the A161 to Epworth, crossing just over the county boundary from Lincolnshire into South Yorkshire and Humberside.

Driving along the familiar lanes around Belton brought back a flood of memories. "This is where I was brought up," I said, slowing the car down as we approached a large detached house, with a petrol garage alongside. "The house was called Axeholme in those days and the only property in the village with a flush loo."

Norman pinched his nose. "Ooh, how posh," he said, in a nasally voice.

"I'll have you know that Granddad Axe was a very well respected man in the area. He even generated his own electricity."

"He must have been a bright spark!"

"Yes, he was," I agreed with a laugh. "Gosh! Central Garage has grown some since my grandfather's day. Wonder what the house is like inside, now?" I pondered, as we drove slowly past the gate.

Norman opened the car window and stuck his head out. "She used to live 'ere!" he shrieked. "Can we come in and 'ave a cup of tea?"

"Norman, stop it!" I said, stamping my foot on the accelerator, just as a man who had been quietly gardening, bobbed his head up over a nearby hedge to see what all the commotion was about.

Speeding away, we giggled like a couple of naughty school kids and I had to stop the car in a lay-by further along the road. "Oh, Norman, you'll get us arrested for breach of the peace," I said, dabbing my eyes with a tissue. "We really must compose ourselves."

In response to my comment, Norman began to wave an imaginary conductor's baton, setting us off giggling yet again.

"Right! Are we okay, now?" I said, checking over my right shoulder before pulling out of the lay-by. We drove on through Belton and I showed him the village shop and Post Office. "The Axe family eventually moved away from the area."

"Well, perhaps they liked to *chop* and change," Norman said, prompting another fit of the giggles.

We intended to leave my car at Norman's flat before flying back to the Isle of Man, so it would be there, conveniently ready for use during any future visits.

Before that, Norman had to make two extra special visits:

the first, for personal reasons, to Bolney, not far from Hayward's Heath.

Norman was excited to learn that his daughter-in-law had just given birth to a baby boy. Gregory was a second child for Norman's son, Nick, and his wife, Kim, and a new brother for Lawrence.

"Welcome to the world, little Gregory," Norman whispered over the side of the carrycot, tears of joy welling up in his eyes as he gazed at his precious grandson.

A Nose for Trouble

Norman's next engagement was at Brinsworth House in Twickenham.

Sometimes known as *Old Pro's Paradise*, this fantastic nursing home is supported and run by the Entertainment Artistes' Benevolent Fund. It is, so I understand, the sole beneficiary of the Royal Variety Performance every year.

Many big-name stars have been past residents at Brinsworth, but it is also for people who have worked in show business in a more behind-the-scenes capacity.

We arrived early for the Celebrity Garden Fete, where Norman was to be the star attraction. "At least they've got good weather," I remarked.

Norman glanced up at the large Victorian house, his expression displaying undisguised affection for the place. "It's always sunny, here," he answered, as if the house itself was to him an old and trusted friend.

"Oh, look Norman! There's Frankie Vaughan and Val Doonican," I said, pointing towards a marquee, where the two stars were chatting amiably.

In truth, there were many other celebrities, yet my memory is a little bit sketchy on that point - if I'd have known that I would one day write a book about my time with

Norman, I should have kept a diary, of course.

Anyway, I'm sure that there were a few side stalls selling yummy-looking homemade cakes and others with plants, bric-a-brac and the like, the atmosphere more akin to a friendly, village fete, really.

I can definitely remember seeing some tables, set out so that the celebrities could charge a couple of pounds for an autograph and then donate the takings to Brinsworth, each one more than happy to support their colleagues.

As a civilian, I noticed how a wonderful feeling of showbiz camaraderie permeated through these proceedings.

Norman spent a lot of time chatting to residents and staff, although, during the afternoon, I'd been vaguely aware that he seemed to be looking out for someone. He obviously hadn't spotted them in the grounds, because he suddenly grabbed my arm.

"Come on, Ann, we're going in," he said, as if we were about to embark on some kind of SAS-style raid.

"W… Why? Where are we going?"

. "There's a special person I want you to see."

As he ushered me along the hallway, Norman glanced left and right, checking in each of the day rooms as we passed. "Ah!" he said, at last, stopping to peer around the door of one particular room.

Sitting in a wheelchair gazing out of the window, was a slim, grey-haired lady with a shawl draped around her shoulders.

She turned as we entered the room, her face lighting up at the sight of Norman. "Oh, I was hoping you'd be here," she said, her voice quivering slightly with age as well as emotion.

"How lovely to see you."

Norman leant over the wheelchair, taking her frail hands in his own and kissing her forehead. "I couldn't come to Brinsworth without seeing my favourite lady, could I?" he said.

Turning to me, he added. "Ann, I'd like you to meet Josie Whittaker, one of my oldest friends and wife of the late, great Eddie Leslie."

"How do you do?" I said.

"And who are you, then, dear?" she asked, her bright eyes looking me up and down.

Before I had the chance to answer Norman hurriedly enlightened her. "Ann is my new Personal Assistant, Josie. You thought she was my bit of stuff, didn't you? Come on, now, tell the truth."

"Well, I suppose I was curious, as she is a very attractive lady."

"Thank you," I said, blushing slightly.

"I thought you might have some nice news for me," Josie continued, glancing down at my left hand. "Something to celebrate, perhaps?"

"Get out of it," snorted Norman.

She wagged her index finger in his face. "You need the love of a good woman, young man. You've been on your own long enough."

"Well, sorry to disappoint you, but Ann and I are not… "

"Someone to take care of you," she butted in, determined not to be 'derailed' from this particular train of thought.

"Ann does take care of me, Josie, and I'm happy enough being single, thank you." He then pressed his nose flat against hers. "Now can we change the subject, please, or shall I wheel you outside and chuck you in the fishpond?"

"Norman!" I said, embarrassed by his rudeness.

"Oh, don't mind us," Josie laughed. "We've always enjoyed teasing one another, haven't we, Norman? Now, come and sit yourselves down, the pair of you."

I pulled up a chair, but Norman started to hop from one leg to the other. "Give me a minute, ladies. I need to go to the toilet, first."

Once Norman had gone, Josie leaned in closer towards me. "Are you married, dear?" she whispered, conspiratorially.

"I'm divorced," I answered, half expecting her to start matchmaking again.

"Children?"

"Yes, a son and daughter, all grown up, of course."

"Well, I should imagine that looking after Norman wouldn't be a suitable job for anyone with a husband at home. Tell me, does he behave himself?"

Josie must have noticed the look of horror on my face, because she burst out laughing. "Oh! I've just realised how that must have sounded. All I meant was, does he behave, or, is he *always playing his silly pranks on you*?"

"Oh, I get plenty of pranks played on me, don't you worry," I answered, joining in with her infectious laughter.

"And how are you settling in?"

"Fine, thank you."

Her face took on an expression worthy of Miss Marple. "Did I just detect a little bit of reticence in that answer, dear? I know that Norman can be a bit, shall we say, stubborn at times."

"No, no, not at all. He's been great, really."

"Yes, Norman is certainly one of the kindest souls you're ever likely to meet," she nodded. "He has been like a rock to me since I lost Eddie, you know. He's the same with anyone who's worked with him, loyal, as the day is long."

"I'm beginning to realise that," I said. "He had a gardener who died a while ago and yet he still goes, once a fortnight, and takes a box of chocolates in to the man's wife at her nursing home."

"How thoughtful of him, though it doesn't surprise me to hear it. He gives of himself, Ann, which is unusual in this day and age. Ah! Here you are, Norman," she said, glancing up. "Better now?"

Norman plonked himself down beside me on another seat. "Yep, smashin', thanks," he glanced at each of us in turn. "And what 'ave you two been gossiping about?"

"Wouldn't you like to know?" Josie chuckled.

It was a real privilege to listen to them both reminiscing about the old times and all the fun they'd had over the years. Immersing ourselves in the stories, we'd quite forgotten about the fete, until Peter Elliott, Chairman and Charity Director, popped his head around the door to say that Norman was needed outside, pronto.

"I've kept you too long," said Josie, patting Norman's hand. "Your fans will be queuing round the block waiting for autographs."

"You mean, my *chums*," Norman corrected her.

Josie was right! After saying our goodbyes to her, we emerged from the house to see that there were hundreds of people milling about, plus, a huge queue, snaking hither and thither across the lawns and out through the gates.

"What's going on?" gasped Norman. "It was a sedate garden fete when we went inside."

"Yes, but I think that they are all here to see you, Normi," I said, feeling slightly overcome when everyone started to cheer.

"Well, in that case, see me they will. Can I have a microphone, please?"

With that, Norman sang a few songs and the crowd loved it. So much so, that they didn't want it to end.

Peter offered to give Norman some sort of remuneration for all his hard work.

"Okay," answered Norman. "Can I have a nice cup of tea and a cheese and pickle sandwich, please?"

That amazing afternoon raised just over £20,000 for the charity and, as we drove away at the end of the fete, Josie's words echoed in my mind… '*he gives of himself, Ann*'.

*

Back on the Isle of Man, things settled down into our normal daily routine, at least for a time.

It seemed to me that no sooner had I washed, dried, aired and ironed our clothes, we were packing our cases again and returning to the mainland. We then drove from Norman's flat down to Southampton, where we were to board The Black Prince for a "Cruise with the Stars".

As one of the "stars" in question, Norman had been booked to do some shows on board. Actually, more like question and answer sessions, really, and this always went down well with the holidaying audiences.

Norman's fellow celebrities on that particular trip were to be Melvyn Hayes and the lovely Johnny Morris, of 'Animal Magic' fame.

We met Patrick on the quayside. "As it's still a bit early, shall the three of us go for a drive before we join the ship?" I suggested.

We hadn't gone far before Norman spotted some cars for sale in a yard. "Stop! Stop!" he shouted. "I want to have a look around."

"Oh, here we go again," I sighed. "I like cars, Norman, but you really are the limit."

"The limit," he repeated, chortling at my unintended pun.

I managed to park nearby. "But remember, Norman, we've only got just over an hour, so don't get too embroiled," I warned him.

It was clear from the look on Pat's face that he was bored by the prospect of watching Norman drooling over yet another flashy car, so I suggested we go for a quick stroll.

On our return, we noticed that Norman seemed to be bending down and taking an inordinate amount of interest in one of the cars. "Whatever is he doing?" asked Pat, intrigued.

"Goodness only knows," I answered. "Perhaps he's been on a test drive and driven it into the wall."

We were still laughing at this rather unsettling mental image, when Norman looked up. "Oh, my God!" I shouted. "Look at his face, it's covered in blood! Oh, Normi, whatever have you done?"

We ran to his side, each grabbing an arm to steady him. "I'm all right, I leapt over the wall and caught me toe, that's all," he said, clearly shaken.

Patrick peered closely at Norman. "You're far from all right, Norman. Here, mate, sit down on the wall."

Norman tried to make light of the situation. "No need to fuss, I'll be fine," he said.

"You're not fine," I told him, dabbing at his face, but the few meagre tissues in my handbag certainly weren't man enough to mop up the copious amount of blood. "I reckon you've broken your nose."

"What are we going to do about the cruise?" I could hear the panic rising in Pat's voice. "Perhaps he needs to go to hospital."

"I'll sort him out, don't worry."

"Well, he can't possibly go on-board in this state. Oh, God, what a mess he's in."

"Pat, calm down, you aren't helping the situation," I snapped.

"Can I be of any assistance?" said a female voice from a house across the road. "Oh, dear me, you'd better bring him inside."

The lady ushered us through to her bathroom and then brought in one of her dining room chairs for Norman to sit on. "I'll fetch some hot water and disinfectant for you."

"Right, Wizzy! Let's get you cleaned up. Honestly, you can't be left on your own for a minute. Isn't it lucky that I'm a qualified First-Aider?" I babbled on, simply to take Norman's mind off the pain.

Ever grateful to that kindly lady for her intervention, we eventually hurried down to the ship, knowing that the question on everyone's lips would be, "Oh, what ever have you done, Norman?"

Mindful of this, the Captain put an announcement out over the Tannoy: *Please don't ask Norman what's happened, coz he's had a bit of an accident, but he's all right.*

"With two black eyes and a swollen nose you look as if you've been in the boxing ring with Frank Bruno, Norman," I told him.

"Yeah, but you should 'ave seen the state of the other fella," he joked, yet I knew that his pride was hurt as much as anything else, having always been so nimble on his feet.

"What do you want me to say to people if they ask me outright how you did it?"

"Tell them the truth, I suppose," he shrugged.

"Really?"

"Yeah, tell 'em that you and Pat beat me up."

"Oh, Norman, people have been giving us funny looks as it is, without putting that idea into their heads," I said. "No, come on, what shall I say?"

He thought for a moment. "That I fell off me bike when I swerved to avoid a dog."

As it happened, the only person who enquired was Johnny Morris. "But I thought you said that you drove down from Epsom?" Johnny said, perplexed. "How on earth did he get his hands on a bike?"

I had no choice then but to tell him the truth. "But please don't let on to Norman that you know," I pleaded.

Thankfully, Norman's injuries healed surprisingly quickly and, yes, before you ask, he did enjoy his trip!

Window Shopping

Norman had many close and valued friends on the Isle of Man.

Robin Oake was the Chief of Police on the island, although, tragically, he and his wife, Chris, sadly lost their policeman son, when he got stabbed in Manchester.

There was beekeeper, Brenda, who made the most delicious homemade ginger flapjacks and, Di and Adrian, who ran the Chablis Restaurant in Castletown.

When I'd first joined Norman, Raina had been the current Mayor on the Isle of Man, whereas her husband, George, had been Mayor the previous year.

I remember that they took us to see 'Singin' in the Rain' at the Gaiety Theatre in Douglas. This was to be the first of many trips to the theatre with the couple, because their son, Gary, was a member of the theatrical group.

Harold Jackson was a builder, originally from Birmingham. Norman used to pop and visit him and his wife, Joan, down at their superb house right by the edge of the sea in Maughold, while I would (quietly!) cook his Sunday lunch back at 'Ballalaugh'.

Over on the mainland, Jeff and Ruby Francis were Norman's very good friends from Solihull and we nearly always broke our journey to Heysham ferry port by staying the night with them.

Back on the island, we paid some very happy visits to Malcolm and Enid's home in the pretty village of Greeba, where Norman and Malcolm would play pool… or, rather, *play* the *fool!*

"Let's leave them to their game," said Enid, during one of our regular Sunday afternoon jaunts over to see the couple. We retreated to the lounge for a cuppa and a chat, although the whoops of laughter emanating from the "games" room were hard to ignore.

"How did that ball get so close to the pocket, Norman?" yelled Malcolm. "It wasn't there a moment ago."

Norman's voice now: "Ooh, um, I dunno, mate. Just a lucky shot, I suppose."

"Lucky shot, my eye. You distracted me and then placed it there."

"Me! Place it there! How can you stand there and have the audaci… the audacitit… the cheek, to accuse an upstanding member of the community like me of such a dastardly thing?"

I soon learned that this kind of conversation (peppered with a few choice swear words, if I'm honest) was the 'norm', whenever Norman played pool or snooker with his friends.

Malcolm owned a garage and first met Norman when he'd called in there to fill-up his car with petrol - I think we've established by now just how fanatical Norman was about cars – and, one morning, Norman cruised into the garage in his much-loved Rolls Royce Silver Shadow, his brow creased with worry lines.

"What's the trouble, Norman?" Malcolm asked. "Is there something wrong with the car?"

"Yeah, there's a rattle in the dashboard that's driving me nuts.

Can you 'ave a look at it for me, please, mate?"

"No problem. It's probably just a loose wire or something."

Malcolm dismantled the dashboard and Norman drove for miles and miles around the island with poor Malcolm crouched down on the floor, listening out for this wretched, barely audible, rattle.

It took a while for Malcolm to fix the problem and so the first thing Norman would say every time he pulled into the garage for petrol, was: "Now, Malcolm, about this rattle… "

*

Remembering Malcolm and Enid Watson has brought to mind The Parish Walk.

This is an eighty-five mile race around the island, with the stipulation that the full eighty-five miles must be completed within a twenty-four hour period, the annual event always attracting athletes and amateurs, alike.

Enid entered, as she had recently taken up race-walking, and Norman's friends, Janet and Roy Dowie, entered us four into the race as well.

"Shall we do a bit of training today, Ann?" Janet asked me.

"I'm game if you are," I said.

Janet turned to Norman and Roy. "And what about you two? Will you be joining us?"

"Yeah, yeah, we will do," Norman agreed. "But… maybe another day."

The guys drove us up over the hill to Port Erin, where they dropped us off. Janet and I then walked the ten miles back home again, much to the astonishment of Norman.

"Well done, girls," he said, admiringly.

Come the day of the race, the plan was for Norman and Roy to walk to the first cut off at the twenty-mile point. However, at around the five-mile mark, Norman began to complain about an ache in his shoulder.

The pair of them went back to Roy's bungalow at St John's, where they played a game of snooker and a game of table tennis. After that, they settled down to watch a football match on telly and then had a little kip. "We'd better go and get the girls," said Roy, finally.

They drove near to the twenty-mile point, surreptitiously parked the van, and race-walked up to the church gate, just four hours after the start.

The media had got wind of the fact that Norman would be taking part and were there to film his "victorious finish", everyone applauding his remarkable "achievement".

Norman, of course, did a bit of method acting, puffing and panting, then bending over and placing his hands on his knees. "Cor! I'm knackered," he uttered, breathlessly.

The organisers awarded them 2nd and 3rd, while the rest of us were still slogging it out around the course.

*

I should have loved to help Norman decorate 'Ballalaugh' that Christmas.

"Do you have any decorations?" I asked him.

"Nah, there's never any point," he said. "I'm always away."

"Ooh, a massive tree would look lovely over in the corner of the lounge," I answered, with a wistful sigh. "But you're right, of course, as no one will be around to see it."

Norman, Pat and I were booked on a Christmas cruise to

Amsterdam. "I never get any time off for good behaviour, you know," I told my sister, Kate, on the telephone.

"Well, look on the bright side, Ann, at least you won't have to cook a Christmas dinner," she pointed out. "Nor do any washing up, either, you lucky thing."

"I know, but I shall really miss seeing you all."

The weather was freezing cold, I remember, and some of the roads from Epsom had a fresh coating of snow.

"It's like fairyland," said Norman, gazing around in wonderment. "All the tree branches are white with frost."

My mood lightened a little as I drove the car onboard the Val De Loire (a super-ferry/cruise ferry), especially when I saw how the decks had been liberally festooned with decorations. And, yes, there was a huge Christmas tree!

A magician performed some impressive close-up magic for passengers during dinner that evening: "Pity you can't conjure us up some decent British food, mate," said Norman, loud enough for everyone to hear.

I nudged his arm. "Norman, behave."

"I can't stand this foreign cuisine," he grimaced, pushing his food aimlessly around the plate with his fork.

"Well, don't you offload it onto me," I warned him.

"Nor me," agreed Pat.

Oh, dear, not a good start to our Christmas celebrations.

En route to Amsterdam I did notice that Norman and Pat were being particularly secretive. "What are you two cooking up?" I asked.

"No… nothing," Pat answered. "Just working out where we want to go when we reach Amsterdam, weren't we, Norm?"

"Yeah, where to go for a bit of… something… food, I mean," Norman chuckled.

"Or an interesting… museum?" Pat stifled a wicked grin.

Norman's blue eyes twinkled with mischief. "In fact, we were hoping to pull a few Christmas crackers whilst we're there."

"Oh, silly me," I shrugged, nonchalantly. "And there was me thinking that you just wanted to leer at the women in the Red Light District."

"What, us?" Norman looked affronted. "We wouldn't dream of it. We think that it's disgusting, don't we, Pat?"

"Oh, yes, I agree," said Pat, his eyes wide with mock horror.

Needless to say, we spent an entire evening traipsing round Amsterdam looking for this notorious area. Much to Norman and Pat's disappointment (and my relief), we never did find the ladies soliciting for business in their brightly lit windows.

"We've been up this street three times already," moaned Pat.

Norman turned the palms of his hands skywards. "We can hardly ask someone for directions, can we?"

"Well, you can, as long as you don't mind ending up with some sort of a sleazy headline in the papers back home," I told him.

Norman nodded sagely and then turned to Pat. "Oh!" His hand flew up to his mouth. "And this means you won't be able to apply for that job you were after, now, mate."

"Job? What job?" Pat asked, perplexed.

"You know, as a window cleaner!"

Vintage Comedy

Last of the Summer Wine was one of Norman's favourite television shows.

He was overjoyed to be offered a part in Roy Clarke's much-loved comedy series. This, though, had all been all arranged in Barbara's time, before I'd started working for Normi.

We were both looking forward to our trip to the beautiful village of Holmfirth in the Yorkshire Dales. Norman was all fired up and ready to play Billy Ingleton in a special episode called, *The Man Who Nearly Knew Pavarotti,* due to be aired the following New Year's Day.

First, we had an overnight stop in a hotel.

I was outside packing the car with luggage the next morning, when Norman suddenly appeared behind me. "What do you think you're doing?" he enquired, brusquely.

"Playing tiddlywinks," I answered, shoving yet another heavy suitcase into position amongst our jigsaw of bags. "Why?"

"That shouldn't go there," he snapped.

"What do you mean?"

He pushed past me and grabbed the cases. "'Ere, leave it to me and I'll show you 'ow it should be done," he said, chucking them down on to the gravel.

"Norman! What are you playing at? I'd just got them in there neatly and now you've… "

"Leave it to someone who knows what he's doing, Ann."

"Whatever's got into you today?" I sighed. "You've been in a funny mood all morning."

I folded my arms and tapped my foot impatiently, but then a little light bulb suddenly switched on inside my brain: "Norman! Some hotel guests are looking out to see what all the fuss is about and I reckon they must be thinking what an unreasonable man you are."

Norman froze. Glancing up at the windows, he saw that a few puzzled faces were, indeed, gazing down at him. Giving each of them a jolly wave, he swaggered round to the front passenger side, opened the car door and jumped in.

"Just have to show him who's boss," I muttered, dusting my hands.

Norman turned in his seat. "'Ere, I'm not deaf, you know."

"No, but you're bloody stubborn," I rejoined.

To his credit, he burst out laughing, but I think that was the one and only time I ever got the last word with Norman!

*

Norman was genuinely thrilled to be on the set of Last of the Summer Wine.

He rushed around shaking hands and generally causing mayhem with the cast and crew, although I suppose it must have been daunting for the established threesome (Bill Owen, Peter Sallis, and, Brian Wilde) to accept a big star like Norman into their midst.

Norman was a little putout to discover that he would not be allowed to tinker with the script. "But I think it would be better if I said this," he suggested.

"No, no, Norman," said Alan J.W. Bell, the show's producer/director. "In television, actors like to keep to the script they've learned."

"But wouldn't it be funnier if… ?"

Alan put his arm around Norman's shoulder and took him to one side. "Listen, Norman, television is a lot different to stage or film work, where seasoned performers like yourself can change the script and ad-lib, but we just don't have the time, with our tight filming schedules."

Norman looked crestfallen. "What if… .?"

"Any deviation from the script would also throw the actors."

"Oh, all right, then," agreed Norman, half-heartedly.

There was one scene where a Jeep was supposed to nearly run Norman over, but he just couldn't resist putting his own particular spin on things. Instead of simply jumping out of the way, as it said in the script, he sprinted off up the lane.

No-one seemed to mind and everyone had a good laugh about it, though.

"I wish I could run like that?" Brian Wilde said to me, enviously. "I'm only seventy and yet I have to use this wretched stick."

"Oh, yes, Norman's very fit for a man in his eighties," I told him. "AND he can still read quite comfortably without glasses."

"That's it! Rub salt into the wound, why don't you?" laughed Brian.

Actually, Norman did get his own way with a few of the scenes. After all, who knew more about slapstick comedy than Norman?

If you recall the bit where Norman's character, Billy, pretended to faint and the paramedics carried him off, it was Norman's idea for Billy to lie crossways on the stretcher, rather than long ways.

They must have liked Norman on Last of the Summer Wine, because he was asked to play a cameo role in the Christmas show, *Extra! Extra!* He made two further appearances in the 2001 series and then another cameo in *Gnome and Away*, later starring in an episode called *The Coming of the Beast*.

Would you believe that during the filming of *The Man Who Nearly Knew Pavarotti* we'd each put on about 5lbs in weight?

Well, the location catering staff kept on insisting that we try some of their irresistible puddings and you can appreciate how one needs to fill up on the kind of foods that stick to the ribs when you're up in The Dales. That's my excuse, anyway!

Norman, of course, was an old hand in these matters and would quickly shed any extra pounds with what he called "D Days" (Diet Days) once back at home. So, I would do the same. In fact, I still put Norman's "D Days" into practice from time to time.

*

Norman was a close friend of producer/director, Alan J.W. Bell, and his wife, Constance.

We went to visit them on a couple of occasions at their beautiful riverside cottage, when we would sit outside on the terrace.

I have this wonderfully poignant memory of Norman standing in amongst Alan's colourful geranium display, miming along to the soundtrack of '*Don't Laugh At Me*' and waving to all the boats. What a surreal image it must have painted for passers by.

Alan and Constance also came over to stay with Norman for the weekend.

"We'll take you up Snaefell," said Norman. "There are some lovely views from up there."

Norman drove over to the Laxey Station and the four of us climbed aboard one of the six wooden railcars to begin our ascent.

"How high is Snaefell?" asked Constance.

"620 metres," I told her.

"That's just over 2,000 feet in old money," said Norman.

"The track is five miles in length, although it seems a lot longer because you're climbing slowly up the mountain," I added.

We stopped at Bungalow Station and I found it strange that Norman didn't tell his usual joke at that point, which was, they called it Bungalow Station, because the builders ran out of bricks and had to bung a low roof on.

The train continued on its way. "That's Sulby Reservoir over there," I pointed, although wisps of grey cloud were now beginning to creep their way across our previously unhindered views.

"Would you look at that?" I sighed, when we finally alighted at the Summit Station, a thick mist now obscuring the much-anticipated vista.

Norman glanced around. "Look at what? There's nothing to see. Oh, and I so wanted to show you the Six Kingdoms: Scotland, England… "

Norman hurriedly turned to me, as if needing my support. "Ireland, Wales, Mann… " I prompted.

"And Heaven," finished Norman, triumphantly.

"Never mind, Normi," I commiserated. "Let's all drown our sorrows with a nice hot coffee in the Summit Cafe."

The lost ball in the gardens at Pinewood Studios. Norman and Sir Donald Sinden at Pinewood Studios. Below. Norman with Lucy Appleby, who played the little orphan girl in A Stitch in Time. Opposite bottom. Norman Wisdom with Sue Benwell, just before his 80th birthday.

Norman with memorabilia at Pinewood Studios.

Norman with Sue Benwell's parents, Tom and her late mother, Lilian, after one of Norman's shows at the Wycombe Swan theatre.

Norman with his crew: Mo (Maureen) the housekeeper, Rodney the gardener and me. This was in 2006 when my role was more carer/PA.

We are in Norman's dressing room on Red Nose Day, before the show on the 1996 tour.

Again in Norman's dressing room, this time after the show.

This was in September 1997 when Marc Sinden, Maurice Bright, John Gatenby and Gareth Hughes came over to the Island to present a cheque for £3000.00 to Norman for his Manx Mencap charity.

One of Norman's 80th Birthday Celebrations with friends. Left to right: Enid, me, Jan and Dianne Norman in the middle enjoying the moment.

Again at his party. He was a great table tennis player which probably explains why the middle is missing from his bat.

Norman adored my poodles Hobo (silver) and Tramp (white).

Norman with my eldest granddaughter Sadie in 1998. He was wonderful with children – they all loved him.

Norman with his dearly beloved grandsons Lawrence and Greg in 1995.

Looking sorry for himself at home.

Taken when my sisters came to stay for a weekend. Joan lives in the States and I am sure spending a weekend at Norman's made her holiday. Left to right: my sisters Kate and Joan, Norman, his Roller, Roy Dowie and me.

Again this time with the dog plus Jan Dowie on the left and Enid on the right.

Norman visiting the Albanian Embassy – with the President.

Johnny Mans with Norman and friends on their return from Albania, when Norman received the Freedom of the City of Tirana.

This page and opposite: Norman in Albania.

Norman in Albania.

Norman celebrating his 80th Birthday at Summerland, Douglas where lots of children were invited to have fun.

Norman and Glenn Ford – the best impressionist of Norman there is. He looks like him too.

Norman, Enid, Jan, Roy and me with a couple of helpers getting ready for the Isle of Man Parish Walk.

Norman with 'Frank Bruno'.

Norman and I about 12 years on from the cover photograph.

Dead-pan humour!

Norman with entertainer Michelle Montuori.

A quiet moment at home playing his piano.

Celebrating his Knighthood at the Thistle Hotel: Clare Spake, me, Norman and his friend Dianna. On the far right is Beckie, wife of Norman's agent Johnny Mans.

Norman tucking into one of his favourite meals.

Joining in with the singing...

Entertaining the ferry crew.

We are amused... Norman with HM Queen Elizabeth II.

Norman with Billy, the Douglas tram horse (above) and opposite driving the tram.

Norman shares his love of speed with motorcyclist Neil Hodgson.

The Icing on the Cake

I found it hard to believe that Norman was about to celebrate his 80th birthday.

"Can we have a shot of you blowing out the candles, please?" said the photographer from HELLO! magazine.

"I'll be out of puff before I blow this lot out," said Norman. "Are you trying to give me heart failure? Yeah, that's it. You're after a journalistic scoop." He turned to me, his face full of mock indignation. "They want a photo of me falling face-first into the cake, Ann."

"Don't even think about it, Wisdom," I warned.

"I wouldn't dream of it," he answered, despite the fact that the thought had obviously crossed his mind.

"You've got enough candles to start an inferno," I laughed.

"Wad do yer mean?" shrieked Norman, tossing his head to one side and doing his best to look affronted by my suggestion. "There aren't *that* many on there."

It really was the most beautiful birthday cake, bought at Harrods and specially presented to Norman by the magazine. Liberally covered with gold-coloured candles, the large, round fruit cake had exquisite white-iced flowers all round the edge.

Earlier in the week, Norman's son, Nick, had telephoned.

"Is Dad within earshot, Ann?" he asked.

"No, you're all right. Why?"

"The family want to organise a party for him, but we shall need to get hold of his address book, so that we can invite all his friends."

"Oh, Nick, there's not many of them left now, as he's outlived everyone. Well, some of them are still alive, I suppose, although you can bet that they won't be as fit and agile as Norman."

(As it happened, George and Raina had arranged a big party for Norman on his return to the island. This was a lavish, sit-down affair at the Hilton on Douglas Prom', attended by dignitaries from the Tynwald, on behalf of the Government of the Isle of Man.

Norman and the Chief of Police on the island, Robin Oake, livened up proceedings by having a bread- roll fight across the room.

"Well, it was an upper-crust affair," Norman pointed out!).

Prior to all this, however, Nick and Kim had organised a Christening party for baby Greg. After the wonderfully heart-warming baptism service we all headed back to their home in Hayward's Heath.

"Surprise!" shouted Jacquie, Nick, and, Kim, in unison, as they opened the front door. They, too, had secretly arranged a party for Norman, who was completely overwhelmed by the lovely gesture.

"This is smashin'" he said, seeing a piano-shaped birthday cake. "And there's me, sitting on me piano stool. How clever is that? I'm a lucky little devil to have such a wonderful family," he added, proudly.

'Ballalaugh' was literally inundated with hundreds of

birthday cards and presents from all over, not just from his fans, but other celebrities. I should know, because I was the one who helped Norman to send out all the thank you letters.

It was truly a labour of love, though… honest!

*

Actually, talking about cakes has brought another typically Norman incident to mind.

Back on the island, Norman was invited to a special celebration for his 80th birthday at Summerland on the end of Douglas prom. Enid was there, as well as about a hundred schoolchildren, invited from all around the island.

The Douglas Corporation presented him with a massive birthday cake and as he was a Patron of Manx MENCAP, Norman decided to donate it to the charity.

Enid and I strolled over to admire the cake. "Oh!" Enid gasped. "Look at that, Ann. We must have a plague of mice in here."

"Actually, I think that it's just *one* mouse in particular," I answered, turning to confront the perpetrator. "Norman! Who's been nibbling round the edge of this cake?"

Norman brushed some imaginary crumbs from the sleeves of his jacket. "Haven't the faintest," he sniffed.

"Well, let's see. It wasn't me and it certainly wasn't Enid. Nor, was it any of these lovely, well behaved children. So, who does that leave?"

"Goldilocks?" suggested Norman, helpfully.

Enid and I attempted to patch things up, by carefully removing bits of the icing from the base and sticking them over the damaged areas. This met with little success, as the once smooth icing was now criss-crossed with fissures.

"It looks like an earthquake zone," said Norman, coming over to inspect our handiwork.

"Yes and whose fault is that?" I answered.

"The San Andreas fault?" he offered, nimbly dodging a cuff round the ear.

Anyway, the recipients at the charity didn't seem to mind, as Norman's "nibbles" simply added to the provenance of the donation, I suppose.

*

Norman used to tour with his hilarious 'Live on Stage' shows every year.

I should guess that most of his fans will have seen him in at various venues across the country. In fact, I reckon that some of them probably knew the script better than Norman!

Norman was assisted by his straight man, Tony Fayne, a tall, suave, pleasantly-spoken guy, who towered above Norman's little Gump character.

Tony's main role was to generally boss Norman around, thus making the audience feel sorry for Norman. Then, he would teach him a 'Lesson in Rhythm' with the notorious 'Biffer and Bonker' machine.

The first thing that had struck me about being away from 'Ballalaugh' for such a long time, was how the fan mail would begin to pile up in our absence.

I had a word with Norman's housekeeper before we left. "Here's the list of theatres, plus the addresses, so can you forward the fan mail to me at each venue, please? Thanks, Mo. Hope it's not too much bother."

"No, not at all, it's a good idea. It'll save you having to come home to a mountain of mail," she answered, kindly.

Norman remained unconvinced. "You won't have time to deal with fan mail," he said, when he saw me loading the typewriter into the taxi.

"Wanna bet? What about when we're travelling between venues or back at the hotel? I'll have plenty of time to kill."

"Oh, yeah, I suppose," he shrugged.

"Listen, Norman, I want to keep on top of all those letters."

"Well, just sit on them, then," he suggested, in his usual helpful way.

Fans regularly wrote to ask if they could meet Norman backstage after his shows and we would always endeavour to write back and tell them to bring a copy of our reply to the stage door, so they could gain entrance.

In fact, despite spending a couple of hours under the gruelling heat of the spotlights, Norman always found time to meet his fans. He would then sign autographs and pose for photos with them, ever appreciative that they had paid to come and see him.

Accompanying Norman on these tours meant I now had to help out with a few little props from the side of the stage.

George, the tour-bus driver, coached me in my duties, which were to include putting a five pound note into Tony's jacket pocket and some cotton wool into Norman's trouser pocket. More importantly, I had to make a quick cameo appearance on-stage.

"We wait in the wings until we hear Tony ask Norman if he can play the drums," explained George. "Then, I'll carry the bigger drum and you, the smaller one."

Shouldn't be too difficult, I thought… mistakenly!

Tony and Norman sat at the front of the tour bus, which had forty seats and a table in the middle, where I would be, typing. As we journeyed along, my 'stage outfits' swung gently to and fro on a rail at the back of the coach.

"What time does the boutique open?" Norman joked.

"I don't want to walk out on-stage wearing crumpled clothes," I told him. "It'll make it look as if I'm living out of a suitcase."

"But you are living out of a suitcase," teased Tony.

"Now, be fair, Tony. Ann has a lot to live up to, what with having to compete with our glamorous George, here." Norman leant forward to pat the driver's substantial stomach. "Especially when she gets concealed behind his huge… drum!"

See what I had to put up with?

During the shows, Norman and Tony did their usual business with the five-pound note.

"Ann!" shrieked Norman, after one particular show. "Tony gave me nothing and I gave him nothing back."

"Oh, I'm so sorry, Norman," I said. "I forgot to put the money in there."

I promised it wouldn't happen again, although I did once forget to give him the wads of cotton wool for his ears. "I was stuffed!" said Norman, crossly. "Or, rather, I wasn't."

Worse was to come, though, when one night George and I were so busy chatting in the wings that we totally missed our cue.

Tony fed his usual line to Norman: "Can you play the drums?"

After waiting patiently for a few moments, Norman finally cupped his hands at each side of his mouth and shouted loud enough for us both to hear. "I CAN, WHEN THEY ARRIVE!"

Some of Norman's fans became regular faces on the tours and would ask if they could carry the drum on-stage. Norman always did this little tug-of-war thing with me, when I went back on to collect the drum, so one chap said, "What should I do if he does that? Should I fall over?"

"No, no," I told him. "Norman's the comedian, leave the pratfalls to him."

Norman always received a much-deserved standing ovation after every single house, even with my unintentional deviations from the script.

*

Norman and I had arrived back at his flat in Epsom one afternoon to the sound of the telephone ringing.

I rushed to answer it before who-ever-it-was rang off. "Oh, hello, Lee," I said. "Is everything all right?"

"Where have you been?" asked my son-in-law.

"We've been to see Norman's good friend, Ruth Gemmett and her son, Dominic, down in Havant," I said. "Why?"

"I've been trying to get hold of you all day," he answered, his tone betraying his anxiety.

"Oh, what's happened? Is Melanie okay?" I was naturally concerned about my daughter, since Mel and her husband had gone through the tragedy of losing a baby eighteen months previously.

"We've had a baby girl," he announced, proudly.

"Oh, that's wonderful. Congratulations!" I turned

to Norman. "Right, Normi," I said. "We're going to Portsmouth tomorrow."

The next day, I drove Norman down to Portsmouth to see the new baby. My sister, Kate, greeted us in the foyer of the Maternity Home.

Once inside the ward, I sat Norman on a chair in the corner. "So no one will recognise you," I whispered to him, pulling his hat lower over his eyes.

Norman behaved himself for all of ten minutes. "Here, Sadie?" He said to my six-year-old granddaughter. "If I buy you a bar of chocolate, will you wear my hat?"

Sadie nodded coyly. "Is it all right if I buy her some chocolate?" he asked Lee.

I suppose the big mistake was allowing Norman out into the corridor. Before I knew it he was tap dancing down the ward and then running around and laughing, sending everyone's blood pressure up sky-high, including mine!

"Norman! This isn't the time or place for your nonsense," I chided. "Oh, I really should have known better with you in tow."

"I thought this was meant to be a *quiet* nursing home," laughed Kate.

"It was," I answered, with a sigh. "Now look at the place. It's more like the set of a Carry On film."

All the nurses gathered round and Norman had to give each and every one of them a kiss goodbye before we could even think of leaving the building at the end of our visit.

"Laughter is the best medicine, Ann," said Norman, when he saw the look on my face.

"They didn't need any medicine till you turned up!"

The next day, one of the other new mums said to Melanie: "Ooh, you'll never guess who was here yesterday?"

"Who?" Melanie asked in an innocent-sounding voice, as if it was the first she'd heard of it. Yeah, right!

*

It always took forever to get a straight answer out of Norman.

I'd asked him several times about the possibility of my two poodles joining us over on the island, but whenever I tried to broach the subject he'd remained non-committal.

I had even written him a little note, although was still none the wiser as to his thoughts on the matter.

The day before we were due to fly back to the Isle of Man, he suddenly piped up. "We haven't discussed your dogs yet, Ann."

"There's nothing to discuss," I said, matter-of-factly. "They're being dropped here in the morning and then I've booked them on to tomorrow's flight… back with us!"

Poodle Parlance

Thankfully, Hobo and Tramp settled in beautifully at 'Ballalaugh' and Norman adored them.

If I was busy in the office I would often hear him chattering to them both out in the garden, where they trotted obediently at his heels.

During our daily walks, they only ever needed leads if there happened to be livestock in the fields. We were strolling along one particular morning, when I noticed that Tramp was missing: "Tramp! Tramp!" we both called, but to no avail.

"I'll go back and find him, Norman."

Norman looked worried. "Where can he be?"

"Oh, he's probably found a rabbit hole, or something. You carry on and I'll catch you up."

I retraced our steps back along the path, calling as I went, until Tramp suddenly dashed out from the undergrowth with a few stray twigs and burrs attached to his coat.

"Where have you been, naughty dog?" I scolded, first removing the uninvited joy-riders from his fur before we could continue our walk. Climbing back up the slope and rounding a bend, I saw Norman lying face-down on the path. "Yes yes, very funny, Wisdom," I sighed.

"I'm not messin'," he said.

I poked him with the toe of my shoe. "No, of course you aren't. Come on, get up, you twerp."

"Honestly, Ann. It's true. I caught my foot in that bramble, there."

Sure enough, as I helped him to stand up, I could see that the left knee of his trouser leg was soaked in blood. "Oh! Norman, what have you done?" I exclaimed. "Come on, I'll help you to the car."

Back at home, I bathed his bloodied knee and Norman removed his sock to reveal a vivid bruise on his big toe. "Ouch!" he said, wriggling it. "See, I wasn't fibbin', Ann."

"Yes, but that's what you get for crying wolf all the time, Normi. No one believes you when you fall over for real."

Later, Norman was eating a piece of my homemade sponge cake.

"Where's Tramp?" I asked him, glancing around the room.

"No idea."

"You've not been feeding him scraps again, have you, Norman?" I enquired, suspiciously.

"No, wouldn't dream of it," he replied. Just then, Tramp's endearing little face popped out from beneath the napkin that was spread across Norman's lap. "Oh!" said Norman, innocently. "How on earth did you get there?"

It was about this time that Norman took a trip out to Chernobyl, to visit the children's hospice set up in his name. Large areas of Russia were still suffering from the devastating after-effects of the world's worst nuclear accident, of course.

I was to stay on at 'Ballalaugh', catching up on the mail

and house sitting, so the dogs would be perfect company for me during his absence.

"It'll seem strange here without you," I told him, as I packed a couple of his warmest jumpers into a small case.

"Don't go having any wild parties while I'm gone," he joked.

"As if," I chuckled. "Though, I can't understand why you don't just fly out and meet the convoy over there, Normi?"

"Because I want to travel with the lads overland and experience everything with them," he answered. "It'd be cheating, going by plane."

"That's very admirable, but it'll be really tough, you know, travelling all those miles in a bumpy supply lorry."

"But not half as tough as life is for those poor kids out there at the moment," he said, pointedly.

It was understandable he should feel that way, because he loved children and hated to think of them suffering. His visits to the orphaned children in Albania had moved him, deeply.

Even whilst away filming Last of the Summer Wine, Norman befriended a fourteen-year-old boy called Ian who had leukaemia.

We went to see him in hospital, where his mother told us that Ian had just undergone an unsuccessful bone marrow operation. "Ian knows that they can't do anymore for him," she'd explained, bravely.

"Yes, but he is going to get better, isn't he?" said Norman, his eyes pleading. "He is, though, isn't he?"

He was shattered when the sad news came through that Ian had died, aged just eighteen, and Norman retreated to his bench in the garden to reflect on the injustices of life. Hobo and Tramp sat patiently at his feet, both gazing up at him as if they understood the reason for his despair.

On a happier note, Norman couldn't resist playing the fool before he left for Russia.

Mo, his housekeeper, was busily vacuuming the lounge, whilst I packed a few last minute food essentials for him to take on his epic trip. As the noise of the vacuum cleaner stopped, Norman suddenly raced out of the kitchen.

"Hey! Where are you going?" I called after him. "We haven't finished here, yet."

I walked out into the hallway, to find him leaning his back against the door of the under-stairs cupboard, Mo's muffled cries coming from within: "Let me out, you b… … !"

I could see that he was up to his usual trick, pinning Mo in there as she tried to put the vacuum cleaner away. "Norman! What on earth are you doing?" I said. "The car will be here to collect you in a minute."

"Don't worry, it's only my old cleaning tart," he answered. This was his naughty nickname for her. "I'll let you out in a mo, Mo," he shouted.

As if that wasn't enough, when Rodney the gardener came in to see him off, Norman scared the life out of the poor man by jumping out from behind the kitchen door.

Oh dear, just a normal slice of everyday life at 'Ballalaugh'. It would certainly be quiet without Norman around to liven things up.

*

The British Comedy Society organised a blue plaque

unveiling for Norman in the Hall of Fame at Pinewood Studios.

The event would benefit one of Norman's favourite charities, Manx MENCAP, but it was also an opportunity for fans and celebrity friends alike to celebrate Norman's Fifty Years in Showbiz.

During the morning's Press Call in Pinewood's gardens, Norman accidentally kicked a football into the pond – the same pond in which he had taken a dip whilst filming Trouble in Store, forty-four year earlier – and he also demonstrated the finer points of how to fall off a bench without injuring oneself.

After all, he was only eighty-two at the time!

There was a Champagne Reception and a luncheon, attended by many of Norman's showbiz pals. These included: Dame Thora Hird, Tom O' Connor and Sir Donald Sinden, as well as Carry On star, Jack Douglas, who was President of the British Comedy Society at that time.

The charity auction raised a substantial amount of money and a month or two later, four representatives from the BCS, Morris Bright, John Gatenby, Gareth Hughes, and Marc Sinden (son of Sir Donald), came over to the island to present Norman with a cheque for £3,000.

"We'll take you both out for lunch," Morris offered.

"Oh, that's kind, isn't it, Norman?" I said.

"Yes… yes, it is," Norman agreed, tugging my sleeve. "But, who are they?" he whispered in my ear.

I said, "Oh, you remember your lovely day at Pinewood, Normi? Well, Morris, John, Gareth, and Marc, have brought your cheque for Manx MENCAP. Isn't that good of them?"

Norman beamed. "Lovely to see you again," he said, shaking their hands.

"Sorry about that," I mouthed to Morris.

"That's okay, don't worry, we understand," he said.

Over lunch, in a lovely Italian restaurant in Douglas, I reminded Norman about his special day at Pinewood. "You played football in the garden, didn't you?"

"Yeah, and I kicked it into the pond," he answered with a chuckle. "And then fell off the bench."

Trust Norman to remember the bits where he'd played the fool!

*

Norman hasn't always played the fool, though.

In the early eighties, his portrayal of a man dying from cancer in the BBC production, Going Gently, received plaudits both from the viewing public and the world of show business.

It was for his dramatic role in an episode of Casualty that his foray into serious acting is most remembered, though.

In the story, *She Loved The Rain*, Norman's screen wife had died and so he wheeled her bed outside, to where the film crew had rigged up a sort of standpipe affair in order to produce the convincing-looking rain effect.

"I hope he can do this in one take," I said. "I don't want him getting a chill."

They did the scene four times and poor Norman was frozen to the marrow, yet, stubborn as always, refused to take a hot shower on site and waited till he was back at the hotel.

His moving, rain-soaked, soliloquy proved to be a most touching moment, despite the fact that Norman had mercilessly tickled the actress's feet to make her giggle all through the intense scene.

Funnily enough, something known as *corpsing* in the industry!

*

One day, Norman went over to London for a charity cricket event at the House of Lords.

I stayed on at 'Ballalaugh' and was busy in the office answering some of his fan mail, when the telephone rang.

"This is the Daily Mirror news desk," said the voice at the other end of the line. "Is Norman Wisdom there?"

"No, he's over in London," I told him.

"Well, we've just heard that he's passed away. Can you confirm that?"

I went cold. "No, I certainly cannot. Who told you this?"

"It came from Parliament," he confirmed.

I contacted Johnny Mans. "I've just had a similar phone call, Ann," he said. "What the hell is going on?"

I was near to tears and spent the entire day pacing around the house waiting for news. "Listen, Ann," said Paul Gaskell's wife, Sue, when I phoned her. "Paul would have let us know by now if anything terrible had happened to Norman."

Johnny phoned the airport. "Sir Norman has just strolled by," said the lady on the Information Desk. "In fact, he's now creating havoc on the concourse."

Yes, Norman was still very much alive. His own take on the matter being that a doorman must have said something like, *Norman Wisdom has passed this way*, which had simply got misconstrued in the confusion.

Now, I wonder who could have caused all this so called 'confusion' in the first place. Hmmm, for the life of me I just can't think, can you?

Still, for all his shenanigans, I gave him the biggest hug and a kiss when he returned home safely later that night.

Petrol Head

Norman was terrible for running out of petrol.

We were driving along the motorway one day, when I noticed a light flashing on the fuel gauge: "Oh, Normi, I told you to stop at the last petrol station." I said to him. "You'd better leave the motorway at this next turn-off."

Suddenly, the display on the gauge changed to a straight line, indicating that the tank was more or less on empty.

"Oh, thank goodness!" I pointed up ahead. "There's a garage."

"Yeah, we should just about make it," answered Norman, the relief evident in his voice.

There was a garage all right: "Oh, no, Norman, it's closed for refurbishments. What are we going to do?"

"Hang on! There are a load of workmen in there," he said, pulling in and parking the car by one of the pumps.

We both walked across to the kiosk and found the lady attendant inside. The next thing I knew, Norman had gone down on his knees in front of her, praying.

"Oh, please, please, give me some petrol," he pleaded.

"Well, I shouldn't really," she laughed. "But seeing as it's you and you asked me so nicely, then I shall be glad to oblige." The kindly lady filled up the car while Norman signed autographs for the workmen.

He loved driving, of course, but had two mishaps in his Rolls Royce. Once, when a Post Office van ran into the side of it and buckled the door. Then, another time, we took the Rolls out to Ballugh Bridge during Race Week and Norman decided to turn right at that point, instead of turning left, as he usually did.

A motorbike came whizzing over the bridge at seventy-miles-an-hour on the wrong side of the road.

"Look out!" I shouted, but, too late.

Thankfully, the French rider was unhurt, but the collision made a terrible mess of the Roller.

We were once cruising along the M6, in order to catch the two o' clock ferry from Heysham. Norman was driving fast, as there was nothing else on the road, although the speed limit was reduced to fifty because of road works.

"There's a police van behind us, Norman," I said, suddenly noticing some blue lights flashing in the wing mirror.

"Oh, that's all we need," he said. "What shall I do?"

"Well, you'd better pull over," I told him.

Norman pulled the car into the road work area and the police van followed, a blue uniform soon looming large in Norman's driver's side window.

"Can you step out of the car, please, sir?" said the stern-faced officer.

Norman accompanied him back to the police van and all went quiet for a while, until I suddenly heard peals of laughter emanating from the vehicle.

He swaggered back to the car and got in. "Well, what happened? Did they book you?" I asked.

"They asked me if I realised that I was speeding," he said.

"And what did you say?"

"I said that I was simply keeping up with the traffic," he answered.

"But there is no traffic," I pointed out.

"Yes, that's what they said."

"Then what happened?"

"They gave me a ticking off and asked for an autograph for their wives."

"Trust you to get away with it, you jammy devil," I chortled.

"Yeah, and I signed them both, *from Speedy Wisdom*."

On another occasion, Norman was driving down a mountain on the Isle of Man. He rounded a bend at the bottom, where the limit suddenly dropped to forty and a policeman pulled him over.

"I won't report you, as you don't want any adverse publicity in the paper, but can I take your particulars?"

"Of course," said Norman, suitably contrite.

"Name?" asked the officer.

"Norman Wisdom!" he replied.

"Address?"

"Ballalaugh, Kirk Andreas."

"And, what do you do for a living, Mr Wisdom."

"Racing driver!"

You see, Norman always had a ready quip to suit any situation.

One night we were on the M25, travelling from Heysham to Epsom. I could see that he was tired, but this was in the days before Norman would allow me to drive his car.

"Normi, let me take over," I suggested.

"Nah, we're nearly home now," he answered, stubborn as usual.

One of Norman's own tapes was serenading us in the car I remember, which may have added to the sleep-inducing effects of the long drive. Not that I'm suggesting for one moment that Norman's music is soporific.

I spotted the brake lights of a car about 180 yards in front of us and shouted for Norman to stop. Norman, however, just didn't seem to register. "Norman! Stop!" I shouted again, my voice rising higher and higher in pitch. "NORMAN… STOP!"

He ploughed straight into the back of this car. "What a berk I am," he said, not really shaken, just more angry with himself, really.

"Yes, you are. You'd better go and apologise to the driver."

Norman went and had a few words and then I got out and spoke to the man.

"You realise who hit you?" I asked.

"Yes," he said.

"Well, he admits full responsibility. We don't really need to involve the police, do we? Shall we just exchange insurance details?"

"I've already called them to get us off the carriageway," he answered.

Norman's car was in a really bad state, with the headlights smashed and the once pristine bonnet all buckled and crushed.

The police advised Norman not to drive the car, but if someone tells Norman *not* to do something, well, you can guess what happened. He started her up and was soon belting along in the outside lane again. "Norman, please take it steady," I said.

"We need to get to Epsom," he insisted. "Our lights might be dodgy, remember?"

We could only have been a couple of minutes into the journey when the bonnet suddenly flew up in front of us, dangerously obscuring our view.

I hit the hazard lights and he hit the brakes, then with my arm stuck out of the window to stop the traffic, we limped across into the middle lane. "I can't see a bloody thing!" Norman yelled. "I'm driving blind."

"Well, I'll be your eyes… left-hand down, okay, stop, that's far enough."

A lorry coming up behind us took a little longer to slow down, but we managed to get over to the inside lane and then, eventually, to the hard shoulder.

"I'll lean on the bonnet and iron out the creases," said Norman. "Come on, you can help."

Consider for one moment the surreal image this must have presented for passing motorists.

Driving along, minding their own business, they suddenly spot Norman Wisdom with an unknown woman at the side of the motorway, bouncing their backsides up and down on the bonnet of a car.

Do you think that anyone actually believed them when they related their story later on? In these days of camera phones, of course, we might have ended up as unintentional stars on YouTube!

I stood back to inspect our handiwork. "Now, Norman, this is no good, just be sensible and let someone else get us home."

"Not likely," he said, stubbornly.

"Why don't you drive on the hard shoulder?" I suggested. "They will excuse us after what's happened."

"No," he said, emphatically.

We began to poodle along in the slow lane at twenty-miles-an-hour, which was absolutely terrifying, what with the traffic entering on the slip roads travelling at speed.

Safely back at the flat, I was just walking through from the kitchen when I overheard Norman chatting on the phone to Phil Day, his publicity guy. "Cor, Phil, you'll never guess what happened tonight? I was in a pile-up on the M25."

"What do you mean, Wisdom?" I said. "You *were* the bloody pile-up on the M25 and if you don't let me drive when you are feeling tired, I shall tell all your friends what really happened."

Norman finished his conversation with Phil. "I'm not trying to bully you, or undermine you, Normi," I told him, giving him a quick hug. "I just want you to allow me to drive when you're feeling tired in future, that's all."

*

Actually, after that little episode, Norman always felt really comfortable with me driving him around and would even drop off to sleep.

One rainy night, we were on our way to Ramsey in the south of the island. "Turn left here," he announced, suddenly.

"Are you sure, Norman?" I said, uncertainly. "I don't remember this road."

"It's a short cut," he assured me.

The wipers were really struggling to sweep the rain from the windscreen and it was pitch dark. The narrow lane seemed to be closing in on us from both sides, until the car tyres eventually ground to a halt in the mud. "So much for your flamin' short cut, Wisdom."

"You won't be able to turn round," he said.

"Wanna bet?"

"There's a field in front of us and drainage ditches on either side, you won't do it."

"Watch me," I said, determinedly.

It was possibly the first ever fifteen-point turn in history, but I finally managed to turn the car around without mishap.

Norman patted me on the back. "You're a sh.. hot driver, Ann," he said, appreciatively, so my skills behind the wheel obviously matched my prowess in the office. Well, in his eyes, at any rate.

*

When I went back in 2005 for my final stint as personal assistant/carer, Norman's health had definitely deteriorated and he was no longer allowed to drive.

Dangerously erratic behind the wheel, he actually scattered some terrified pedestrians on a zebra crossing, so that his family feared that it would only be a matter of time before he killed himself and/or someone else.

At first, we all thought it better to keep his cars, so that Norman could still own and admire them, but I soon discovered that this was a bad idea.

"Come on, Ann," Norman would say. "Give me the car keys. I'm capable enough to drive."

"No, you're not, Norman. You had a test and failed it, remember?"

"I *did not* fail it," he'd insist.

"I've given your car keys to the police," I lied.

Norman would then ring Marion, who was in charge of the

tests, to try and cajole her into letting him get back behind the wheel again. I asked her if she would be good enough to send Norman a letter, explaining once and for all why he was not allowed to drive.

"At least then, when he asked me for the car keys, I can show him your letter," I told her. If that didn't work, I'd then ring the local police station to ask if someone would pop round and have a chat with him.

"Give me my keys back," Norman used to say to the police.

"Oh, we've sent them over to the mainland," they told him, now complicit in my fib. "Just be happy," they said, but it must have been so frustrating for Norman, because cars were his life.

I phoned Nick one morning, when Norman was out of earshot. "Yes, it would be kinder if we sold them," he agreed. "They are just a tantalising temptation for him, sitting in the garage."

Anyway, Malcolm dispatched them while Norman and I were away on a cruise.

Before that, Nick had arranged with Malcolm to get us a smaller car, as I wouldn't drive Norman's Jaguar, and he got a Ford KA. Norman was really happy to be driven around in that and had no ambition to drive it himself, because it wasn't racy enough for him.

Norman never let poor Nick forget that he'd sold his precious cars, though, despite the fact that it was done with his best interests at heart.

Thanks for the Memories

October 2010

I retired five times from my wonderful job as Norman's personal assistant.

The first time was in February 1999, on my sixtieth birthday, although I was only home for a couple of months and then I went back again. I had the longest break after the fourth time, between 2002 and 2005.

Norman's health had deteriorated by that time and so my role was more carer, than personal assistant. He really seemed to improve for a while and people would ring me up and say that he was back to his old self again.

To make things easier for me, his family arranged for us to go away on several cruises, with one of them lasting four weeks, when Enid joined us.

The on-board pianist, Emile, was wonderful with Norman and picked up his tunes really quickly. Norman used to make me laugh when he referred to him as Email.

"His wife is called Dot Com, you know," he'd joke.

Norman's short-term memory may have been failing, but he never forgot the words to his songs, especially the one that will forever be associated with him, *Don't Laugh at Me*.

Now, I am standing with Norman's family and a few of his closest friends, as he is finally laid to rest.

If only he could have seen all the people who turned out to line the streets of Douglas for him on his final journey and hear all the lovely things said about him in the church service.

Yes, everyone loved him.

Ever grateful to his family for asking me to join them today on this intimate occasion, I throw a single rose into the grave, which lands softly on the coffin lid.

Then, through a blur of tears, my mind suddenly travels back over all the happy times I spent in the company of this extraordinary man…

*

Do you remember that occasion when your lovely family came over to stay with us at 'Ballalaugh', Normi? I think Greg, your grandson, was about eight-years-old.

"Look, Granddad!" he said, pointing at the lounge carpet. "The dog's done something on the floor."

"Ann!" you shouted.

I'd rushed in, armed with some tissues and full of apologies, only to find that it was a pretend dog mess that Greg had purchased from a joke shop in Douglas that very morning.

Like grandfather, like grandson!

What about the time that Jacqui's seat belt snapped and you painstakingly cut out some cardboard and painted it black? No one could spot the difference, although it was a bit naughty, I know. "Needs must," you'd said.

Do you remember when we went to Liverpool and you visited those two little girls in hospital? A life-saving regime of chemo -

therapy had robbed them of their beautiful blonde hair and they only had a few strands left between them.

How it broke your heart to see that, but you never let on and just concentrated all your efforts into cheering them up.

The same thing happened when we went to Frank Carson's 80th birthday bash out in Northern Ireland. Frank took you to meet a young woman who was suffering from terminal cancer. She had two young children and your surprise visit to the hospice meant everything to her.

I will never forget when we went to Westminster Abbey for the Bravest Children Awards. We had problems finding a parking space and so we drove up to the gates of the House of Lords to ask a policeman.

"Oh! Norman, how nice to see you," he said, before kindly directing us to a space in the House of Lords car park.

We were so impressed with the Duchess of Kent, weren't we? How she would sweep all those little children into her arms and give them a hug.

It was an extremely moving occasion and when you caught me dabbing my eyes with a hanky, you reckoned the makers of Kleenex Tissues must have made a fortune that day.

"It's not to be sneezed at," you'd said.

What about that time we went to Dublin for the Classic Car Show? We had an Army escort, which was a good thing, or we might have been crushed in the crowds, so pleased were they to see you. We stayed at the Mansion House and you slept in the same bed as had been slept in by President Kennedy and The Pope, no less.

Funnily enough, you didn't ask me to swap rooms that time!

We then had a police escort to the airport and arrived so early that we had to wait an age for our flight. You didn't mind, though, did you? As it was a golden opportunity to lark about with the other passengers.

Another lovely memory is when you were a guest on the Noel Edmonds House Party programme, along with the Spice Girls and Ronnie Corbett. The girls' wanted your autograph and, in return, I received two signed photographs of them, one for Sadie, my granddaughter, and one for Lucy, Johnny Mans' daughter.

I have to smile when I think of poor Ronnie, waiting patiently in the bar for the next car to take him home. You walked straight past him, oblivious, and took his car, leaving me to apologise on your behalf.

I remember how devastated you were when I had to have Hobo put to sleep. Even though he was seventeen-years-old, and blind and arthritic, you never did forgive me for that.

What about that time all the electricity went off at 'Ballalaugh' and we were suddenly plunged into darkness?

"I'll go out and check the fuses," I said, grabbing my torch, only to return to find you lying rigid on the hall floor, your hair spiked up, as if you'd been electrocuted.

You were lovely to my sisters, Kate and Joan, when Joan came over on a visit from the States. "Come and stay at 'Ballalaugh'," you told them, generously.

They enjoyed themselves so much, Normi, although I don't think they've ever recovered from that white-knuckle ride you gave them in the BMW840!

I remember coming home from a walk one day, to find you anxiously pacing the living room: "Your… sister, Kate…

phoned," you stammered, avoiding my eyes. "She said that… her father… has died."

You just couldn't bring yourself to tell me the terrible news about my dad, could you?

What about the time we went to Liverpool for a special luncheon with Howard Keel? The photographer asked if I was Mrs Keel, which I was most flattered about, as he was an extremely handsome man.

"Oh, yes," you said to him. "Her first name is Eve and her middle initial is 'N'." Honestly, Norman, *Eve N. Keel*, indeed.

One afternoon, we were just leaving Mel's house, when you suddenly spotted the lady who lived opposite, standing on her doorstep with her son and daughter.

They were there to wave you off, but you ran over and chased those delighted children up and down the stairs and back out into the garden again. How thrilled they were to think that Norman Wisdom had actually been inside their house.

You loved your Film Festival at the Barbican, which was a really special event spread over three consecutive days.

Also, the Heritage Foundation organised that 'Lifetime Tribute' luncheon in your honour at the Grosvenor House hotel in London. You'd been an annual President of the charity back in 1996, when it was known as Comic Heritage.

The prestigious event was attended by the Albanian Ambassador, Mr Agim Fagu, along with many famous faces from the world of showbiz.

The Chairman of the charity, David Graham, waited for you in reception, but instead of using the more sensible side-door entrance, you made straight for the revolving doors. Oh,

Normi, you went spinning round and round, until you finally shot out into the foyer like a cork from a bottle of champagne, much to the surprise of some American hotel guests.

You then spotted Sir Alex Ferguson and a few of the Manchester United players, like David Beckham. I think that they were attending a private reception there, before playing a match against Arsenal the next day.

Sir Alex was busily embroiled in something when you rushed past him, performing one of your customary trips as you went by. Sir Alex, though, didn't seem to notice.

You tripped again and yet Sir Alex, who by now was beginning to look slightly peeved, still carried on with what he was doing.

Unperturbed, you tripped again, only this time you sprawled right across the table in front of him.

"Ah! It's you, Norman!" said Sir Alex, immediately forgetting his former irritation and embracing you like a long-lost brother.

You could get away with anything, couldn't you, Normi?

We used to be invited to the Queen's garden parties and goodness only knows what you were whispering to Prince Andrew one year, but whatever it was sent him into fits of laughter. Another year, you and Jeremy Spake had massive queues of people waiting for autographs, didn't you?

Later, when I was between stints as your personal assistant, Jeremy stayed at my place for a few weeks whilst he was in pantomime down in Fareham.

We discovered that you were in hospital and so Jeremy and I tried to pop in and visit you, but the sister refused us entry. We were about to leave, disappointed, when you overheard us talking in the corridor. You insisted on seeing us and the nurse brought you out in a wheelchair.

Everyone felt really proud when you were awarded your O.B.E. and even more so, of course, when you went to Buckingham Palace to collect your Knighthood.

You just couldn't resist doing one of your trips in front of the Queen, though, could you, *Sir* Norman?

Yes, I have a treasure-trove of memories, thanks to you.

Normi, I want you to know how grateful I am for the kindness you've shown to me and my family over the years and to say how much I admire all the wonderful things you achieved in your long and eventful life.

This book is my tribute to you and whenever I'm feeling down, I shall remember your little rhyme:

> Let laughter make the world go round,
> Such is life and life is such
> And after all it isn't much,
> First a cradle, then a hearse,
> It might have been better
> But it could have been worse!

God bless.
Your loving secretary bird, Ann xx

****

Little Big Man

The above was the title of an article I wrote about Norman Wisdom, published to coincide with his 80th birthday in February 1995

What a joy to sit face-to-face with this iconic comedy star, drinking coffee and chatting about his life. I will treasure the memory forever.

I wrote a further three pieces about Norman, including a report about the British Comedy Society's tribute and plaque unveiling for him in Pinewood's 'Hall of Fame'.

It was during the very first interview at his flat in Epsom that I met his capable Personal Assistant, Ann Axe. We were then destined to bump into one another at various charity events, organised by the BCS and the Heritage Foundation.

Ann also kindly arranged for my parents to meet with Norman back-stage at the Wycombe Swan theatre, after one of his 'Live on Stage' shows, yet another much-treasured memory.

In subsequent years, Ann and I exchanged Christmas cards. Then, one day, she phoned to ask if I would be interested in writing a book about her life with Norman. It has been an absolute privilege, Ann, and thank you for entrusting me with the task.

Sadly, of course, Sir Norman died during the writing of this book.

There are certain special people who can touch the lives of others and make a difference to the world. Norman Wisdom was such a person.

I can only end this piece with a quote from the final line of my article about him: **thank you for the laughter... and the tears, Little Norm'.**

Sue Benwell.